Living With Integrity
Unitarian Values and Beliefs in Practice

Edited by Kate Whyman

The Lindsey Press
London

Published by the Lindsey Press
on behalf of the General Assembly of Unitarian
and Free Christian Churches
Essex Hall, 1–6 Essex Street, London WC2R 3HY, UK

© General Assembly of Unitarian and Free Christian Churches 2016

ISBN 978-0-85319-088-2

Designed and typeset by Garth Stewart, London

Printed and bound in the United Kingdom by
Lightning Source, Milton Keynes

In memory of Kate Taylor

Contents

Introduction

Kate Whyman

Faith is not an abstraction, but a way of living.
(Palfrey Perkins)

The first Unitarian service that I ever attended, in Brighton in July 1999, included the hymn 'Others Call it God' (written by William Herbert Carruth; number 233 in *Hymns For Living*). But I was quite unable to sing it. The idea that God might be encountered in the 'high yearnings' of our hearts, in 'a picket frozen on duty' or 'a mother starved for her brood' literally took my breath away and filled my eyes with tears. If pressed to identify what it was about Unitarianism that first slipped under my sceptical radar and punched me in the solar plexus, then I would say that was it. The words spoke to me of a divine power that finds expression through each one of us when we dare to live fully and fearlessly from the depths of our hearts and souls; when we willingly make sacrifices out of love and concern for others; and when we allow ourselves to be guided by spirit rather than merely by ego – in other words, when we live with integrity.

When I took on the task of commissioning this book, which grew out of an original idea by Derek McAuley (Chief Officer of the General Assembly of Unitarian and Free Christian Churches), that same hymn must still have been ringing in my ears. I was excited by the idea of different Unitarians, with their various beliefs, sharing the particular words, music, and theology that had inspired them and motivated them to live the way they do. And I wanted to hear about the inevitable difficulties of attempting to integrate faith and values with real life choices, and how and why the struggle was worth it. I hoped that the results would challenge and inspire me and, by extension, readers of the book.

How to do it? Collectively the Lindsey Press Panel came up with twelve themes which spanned different stages of life and included some of its major preoccupations and ethical dilemmas. Between them the chapters of this book address aspects of personal and home life, such as navigating personal relationships, bringing up children, coping with loss and dying; ways of engaging with the wider world, for example, in the workplace, in the political arena, and on the campaign trail; and responses to pressing global issues, such as migration and abuse of the environment.

The next task was to set about identifying Unitarians who could write authentically from their own life experience. I have been conscious of trying, as far as possible, to find a balance between women and men, ministers and lay people, experienced writers and those who have never been published before, and to include a range of beliefs and theologies. There are also some younger contributors and a degree of geographical spread (although I am aware that there is no real cultural diversity here, a limitation which I hope will be redressed in future publications). The result is that the chapters, perhaps not surprisingly, are very varied in style and approach – even though the authors were all given the same style brief.

This is not a book that tries to tell you how to be a Unitarian, or how to live a good life, or even what it means to live with integrity – there could be no such book, or at least not one that itself had integrity. But it is an attempt to show how *some* Unitarians engage with key elements of their lives in ways that resonate with their beliefs, their values, and their faith. This book presents no stated theology, ethic, or set of values of its own, but instead provides space for its authors to name their own sources of religious and spiritual inspiration and tell us how these core ideas have informed their way of life, and how they continue to do so. Each chapter is a very personal testimony and is intended to serve not as a model but as a springboard for reflection. To this end, the contributors also offer suggestions for further reading and questions for discussion.

Re-reading the book now, in its final form, I am struck not only by the rich diversity of the voices but also by an underlying coherence. These contemporary women and men, each with their own influences and beliefs, each with their unique set of life experiences and very personal approaches to life's challenges, nevertheless seem to add up to something bigger than the sum of their parts. They seem, to me at least, to encapsulate a very Unitarian way of approaching life, in all its complexity and mystery: a way of profound thoughtfulness, questing intelligence, and passionate determination. They are honest and often brave, and I hope that their examples will prompt each of us to consider how we strive to make our faith 'not an abstraction, but a way of living', for the benefit of all our futures.

I would like to thank all the members of the Lindsey Press Panel for their invaluable input and support, particularly the late Kate Taylor for her enthusiasm for this project, and Catherine Robinson for copyediting the text and overseeing the production of the book. Finally, my sincere thanks to each and every one of the contributors for giving so generously of their time – and of themselves – to make this book possible.

Kate Whyman
January 2016

(Revd. Kate Whyman is the Minister of the Unitarian Church in Plymouth and Pound Square Unitarian Chapel in Cullompton.)

Part 1: Doing the Groundwork

Navigating relationships and sexuality

Stephen Lingwood

Introduction: Unitarians and sex

Sex and religion: two topics not to be mentioned in polite conversation, and especially not together! These two topics, which have always fascinated me, are often kept apart at arm's length. Even within the liberal tradition of Unitarianism, very little has been written about the intersection of the two. I am not aware of the Unitarian tradition having a lot to say on the subject of relationships and sexuality. A good summary of recent thought is Ann Peart's essay 'Of Warmth and Love and Passion: Unitarians and (Homo) sexuality'.[1] But, as the title suggests, this is largely about homosexuality and only partly about sexuality in itself.

This has often been the case for Unitarians. We have made great strides in advocating the acceptance of gay, lesbian, and bisexual people in the Unitarian community. However, this progress has not really been accompanied by any serious reflection on sex and relationships as such. For example, we have recently campaigned successfully for marriage equality in England, Wales, and Scotland; but the General Assembly motion promoting this initiative was written in terms of a liberal-secular/human rights/equality framework. At no point did we stop to ask: is marriage an inherently good thing? Do we believe it to be so? Why? In other words, we said 'We believe in marriage equality' without considering whether we could say 'We believe in marriage'.

---

1   See Peart (2003).

Do we believe in marriage? What would that mean? Does Unitarianism have anything useful to say about what makes a good marriage – or a good sexual relationship – or good sex?

In broad terms, the answer is No. Beyond our generally liberal instincts we have no in-depth theology or ethics on sexuality and relationships. Nor is there room within these pages to develop one. I believe that this work should be done in the future, but that is not what this is. This is an entirely personal reflection on how I, as a committed Unitarian, navigate my sexuality and my relationships.

My perspective

I write from a limited perspective. I can only write as a cisgender,[2] white, British, bisexual,[3] single man. The one word that jumps out at me from this list is *single*. It could be judged that, as a 33-year-old single person, I have *failed* in the task of sexuality and relationships, as I have not succeeded in forming a long-term relationship or marriage at this point in my life. So who am I to wax lyrical on this subject? I certainly feel inadequate to the task.

All I can do is reflect on my life and briefly highlight some of the values and theology that I try to bring to my sex life and personal relationships. This attempt must inevitably be partial and a work-in-progress. It also risks accusations of hypocrisy. As I expound these ethical values, it is possible that some ex from my past might say, 'Well you didn't live up to those values *then!*' Or that some possible future partner might read this and hold me to account for the values that I have espoused! There is no escaping the danger of hypocrisy here. I can only beg for grace and forgiveness as I try, as we all do, to struggle through the messiness of life.

---

2   'Cisgender' refers to a person whose gender identity matches the body that he or she was born with, as opposed to a 'transgender' person, who experiences a mismatch between the body he or she was born with and his or her gender identity.

3   I have written about my bisexual identity in 'Bi Christian Unitarian: A Theology of Transgression' in *Sexuality, Religion and the Sacred: Bisexual, Pansexual, and Polysexual Perspectives* (Abingdon: Routledge, 2012).

The holiness of the intimate and the intimacy of the holy

The place from which I start in my theology is a commitment to the holiness of the intimate and the intimacy of the holy. By this I mean that God is not far away or abstract, but deeply intertwined with (or synonymous with) everyday reality. Another word for this is incarnation ('infleshment'). The person who expressed this best for me is the poet Walt Whitman, when he wrote: 'The scent of my armpits is purer than prayer.'

The holy is intimate, nearby. The word 'intimate' of course also draws our minds towards sex. Sexuality, as part of the physical world imbued with the presence of God, is ultimately good. In biological terms, of course, it is an astounding and miraculous mechanism for the perpetuation of the species. While I would not want to devalue the importance of this, I must say that sex is also a great deal more than that.

Sexuality begins with a relationship with our own bodies. My Unitarian commitment to the intimacy of the holy means that I don't ignore my body as an important part of my self. My basic ethical commitment to 'love my neighbour *as I love myself*' means that I must love myself, including my body. I have not always found it easy to love my body, which perhaps is true for all of us. We are surrounded in our culture by myriad images of 'ideal' bodies, which we can rarely live up to. Although women's bodies are displayed, commodified, and objectified more than men's bodies, this process does affect us all. In adolescence I was suddenly lumbered with this strange, flabby, bumpy, hairy adult body, as are we all. I think it takes years (if not decades) for us to get really used to having an adult body. It takes a long time to overcome the adolescent shame that many of us feel for our bodies – if we ever do.

In the Book of Genesis, Adam and Eve go through a similar development of self-consciousness and become 'naked and afraid'. How many of us are still 'naked and afraid'? But my faith calls me to return to this original Eden state of being naked and unashamed. My incarnational Unitarian theology urges me to make friends with my body and to love it. While I still want to 'make the best' of my body and appearance in reasonable ways, I do not hate it or want to radically change it. Unnecessary cosmetic surgery would not be consistent with this spiritual approach to my body.

I think that it is only in my thirties that I have become truly comfortable in my own skin. Only now have I learned to love my body, to have the capacity to be naked and unashamed. This attitude is an inseparable part of my spirituality.

The desire for intimacy with the other

Although sexuality begins with a relationship with our own bodies, for most of us it does not end there. In Genesis we are told that creation was 'good', and the first thing that was 'not good' was that Adam was alone. As a Unitarian I believe that disconnection, alienation, aloneness is in many ways *the* problem. Physically, psychologically, sociologically, and theologically our problem is alienation.

We need connection. One of the places where we find connection is in human emotional intimacy. We find this emotional intimacy in those relationships where we feel we can 'really be ourselves'. Research shows that we value such relationships most highly and find them to be the most nourishing.[4] While such relationships can often come in the form of sexual relationships or marriage, they can also come in other forms, including friendship.

In my life I have had to slowly learn to understand my deep need for intimacy. If I go more than a week without intimacy, without spending time in the company of people where I feel I can truly be myself, then I can feel my mental health suffering. If I go more than a week without a pint with a mate or a good chat with a loved one, then I feel my mood darkening and my energy levels dropping. I need – almost bodily need – that experience. And the experience must be physical, not an online conversation or chat on Facebook. I need to breathe the same air and share the same physical space with another in order to feel that deeper connection.

4   Barker (2012), p. 17.

But friendship does not always feel sufficient. And so I date, as I have done for years. There are times, though, when the process of dating feels exhausting. Dating involves commitment. Dating (particularly using dating websites) is a lot like looking for a job. You have to fill in your CV, make the most of your attributes (without appearing arrogant), make applications, and (if you're lucky) get an interview. Just as being unemployed and going through this process again and again can be deeply disheartening for the unemployed job-seeker, so it can for the single dater.

Is there an alternative? I don't present myself as any kind of expert, or someone who has this stuff 'sorted', but more recently I have been trying to shift my thinking around this. Instead of a desperate search for one person to 'solve' my need for intimacy, I pray that I can be open to all the ways in which I can be open to deeper connection, while resisting expectation of the forms within which that connection might come.

This means that I try to nurture deep friendships, put myself in situations where I will meet lots of new people, and notice when I feel some connection with a person, to make a commitment to get to know them better. I keep my eyes open to the possibility of connection, whether that is one date over coffee, one encounter in a nightclub, or even the simplicity of sharing a friendly word with someone while queuing for a train ticket. And I try to do this without expectation or projection of what this might lead to in the future. In other words, I try to be *open* to the possibility of connection and intimacy, sexual or otherwise, without *grasping* for it. I try not to control or predict the future, but keep my eyes open to the situations and the people that I think might be *life-giving* for me. I would still like a lifelong sexual relationship, a marriage, but I try to be open to ways in which my need for intimacy might be met in myriad different ways beyond the traditional model.

When I do find myself open to sexual intimacy and relationships I try to be guided by the ethical commitments of my life as a Unitarian. What are those ethical commitments? Or, to put it differently, what makes sex 'good'?

What is good sex, and when is sex good?

Good sex is equal

Equality is essential for me. This includes a commitment to equality of the sexes. As a bisexual man (and someone who deliberately embraces the label 'queer'), I tend to resist gender stereotypes. I am a feminist, not simply out of a wish to be an ally to women (although I hope I am), but also because I believe that sexism and misogyny harm men too. I am frustrated by expectations of how the man and the woman should behave in a dating situation or relationship. If I date a man, there is a natural equality and unique negotiation of roles, based on the individuals involved. But if I then date a woman, it feels as though I am operating under a set of conventional rules or expectations. Such expectations might be something as simple as 'the man pays for the meal', but such expectations disturb and frustrate me. If I date a man, there is no expectation that I should necessarily pay, so why should it be different if I date a woman?

Equality also includes a commitment to professional boundaries. As a minister I believe it would be entirely inappropriate for me to have any kind of sexual relationship with someone in my congregation or anyone with whom I have a professional pastoral relationship. Such a relationship would be unequal, because as a professional minister I am in a position of power, and there would be potential for manipulation and abuse of that power by virtue of my position if sex became involved. Sex that involves an imbalance of power is, clearly, not ethical sex.

Good sex is pleasurable

This might seem obvious in some ways and not really a question of ethics. But it is. Many have pointed out that we live in a 'rape culture', and in response to this there have been concerted campaigns to change the approach to rape in our legal system. Instead of 'No Means No', the onus is changing to 'Yes Means Yes' and anything else is rape, recognising that if a victim is drunk, unconscious, incapacitated, or too frightened to speak, that is not an excuse for rape.[5] The way to change this in our culture is for us all to look for an enthusiastic 'yes!' in our sex lives. But it takes courage to say, 'I like that' or 'I don't like that, stop doing it', or 'Do you like that?', or 'Would you like me to do this?'

Pleasure and mutual concern are not just for the moment of sex itself, but are important in the long run too. The flip-side of the commitment to pleasure is the commitment to do no harm. Long-term unpleasurable consequences should be avoided. One aspect of this is the commitment to stop the spread of sexually transmitted infections. For me, a non-negotiable commitment is to practise safe sex, as well as getting tested for sexually transmitted infections on a regular basis, for my own health and for the health of others. It is not particularly pleasant, but for me as a sexually active person I believe it is deeply important to get a sexual health check-up at least once a year.

Good sex draws us into deeper communion

Sex is one of the most profound ways in which human beings connect with one another, creating intimacy, cementing relationships, and expressing love. There is a synergy in which two become one in a way that dissolves the boundaries between 'me' and 'you'. There is something uniquely powerful about two people who are sharing not only their bodies, but also their lives. There is something special about sex that comes through deep knowledge of the other, their body and their soul: out of a deeper sharing, love, and knowledge of one another.

However, the communion of sex is not limited to stable, long-term loving relationships or marriage. Deep communion, the synergy of connection, a mutual concern for another, and the giving and receiving of pleasure are also possible in an encounter with a stranger that lasts for two minutes. There are of course increased dangers of misunderstanding, selfishness, and just plain awkwardness in a casual sexual encounter, but nothing that inherently makes such an encounter unethical or unspiritual.

---

5   http://www.telegraph.co.uk/news/uknews/law-and-order/11375667/Men-must-prove-a-woman-said-Yes-under-tough-new-rape-rules.html (accessed 30/06/15).

Good sex is truthful

Inspired by the command of Jesus 'to let your yes be yes and your no be no',[6] I am committed as a Unitarian to speaking truth plainly. The temptation in the world of dating is to be 'economical with the truth' in presenting our best side to potential partners. I don't believe it is possible to lay down strict rules about this, and there is no need for 'full disclosure' of every aspect of oneself straight away (that would surely be frightening for anyone). But pretending to be something that you are not is ultimately counter-productive. So, for example, on my online dating profile I don't say that I am a minister, but I do say that I am a Unitarian and that my faith is a big part of my life. I used to avoid saying this for fear of putting people off (today religious faith is regarded as a pursuit for a strange minority), but now I am much more open about needing to share that part of me with someone who could become a part of my life. Shame has no place here.

Nor is it appropriate to engage in sexual acts that involve dishonesty or deceit relating to any third party. It is not unusual on a dating website for me to be approached by a married man seeking an illicit encounter, without the knowledge of his wife. I ignore such messages. However, I am aware of the fact that for many people relationships overlap, and one relationship starts while the other is dying. While not endorsing this, I try not to be judgmental of others.

Truthfulness involves confronting truth as well as speaking truth. I was once in a relationship where in a period of a few weeks my partner persistently failed to turn up for arranged meetings, did not return calls, and just seemed generally distant. It took several weeks of this for me to accept the truth that this was probably because he wanted to end the relationship, but was not brave enough to say that outright. He certainly should have taken responsibility for his feelings and spoken the truth. But I also learned that I should have taken responsibility in confronting the truth much earlier and saying, 'This behaviour is unacceptable. You're

6   Matthew 5, verse 37.

acting like you don't want to be in this relationship. If that is true, please tell me, to spare both of us valuable time and unnecessary pain.' The truth is sometimes hard, but it is better than living a lie.

Navigating relationships, sexuality, and singleness

Despite the popular cliché about bisexuals getting a lot of sex, the fact is that I have spent the vast majority of my life single, and a good proportion of that celibate. I am largely content with my life, but I am still drawn by a desire for intimacy, and for sharing a lifelong monogamous union with another person. I try to hold on to this desire lightly, while opening my life to love in myriad ways: through friends, family, community, ministry, encounters with others, and ultimately with the Beloved. Though I need that Love to be incarnated, infleshed, I will always return to the ultimate source of all love, the God of my heart, my Beloved.

Questions for discussion and reflection

1. How would you describe your relationship with your body? As a friend? An enemy? A companion? A vehicle? Or something else?

2. Do you think that sex is a topic that we should discuss more in religious community? What might be the challenges and rewards of doing so?

3. What ethical commitments should we apply in our relationships? What are your commitments? Do you think they are purely personal, or can they be applied to all people?

4. Do you see a link between sexuality and spirituality? How are they the same and how are they different?

Further reading

Barker, M. (2012) *Rewriting the Rules: An Integrative Guide to Love, Sex and Relationships*, Hove: Routledge.

Lingwood, S. (2012) 'Bi Christian Unitarian: A Theology of Transgression' in *Sexuality, Religion and the Sacred* (Abingdon: Routledge) (and available by request from the author).

Peart, A. (2003) 'Of Warmth and Love and Passion: Unitarians and (Homo) sexuality' in *Unitarian Perspectives on Contemporary Social Issues*, London: Lindsey Press.

Williams, R. (1989) *The Body's Grace*, London: Lesbian and Gay Christian Movement.

The author

Stephen Lingwood is the Minister of Bank Street Unitarian Chapel in Bolton, Lancashire. He is a chaplain at the University of Bolton and was instrumental in founding Bolton Street Angels, an ecumenical ministry to the nightlife of Bolton town centre. He holds degrees from the universities of Birmingham, Boston (USA), and Manchester. His interests include bisexual and queer theology, and Unitarian theologies of mission and evangelism. He is the Editor of *The Unitarian Life: Voices from the Past and Present* (Lindsey Press, 2008). In 2015 he was named a GLBT Christian Role Model in a publication by Stonewall.

Nurturing our children

A conversation with
Claire and Josh Hewerdine

Fundamental principles

Claire: My Granny once said to me that the key to bringing up children is giving them firm roots and strong wings. If you manage to do that, then you have done a good job. She was an Anglican, like most of my recent ancestors, although I can't remember her talking much about religion. I do, however, remember those words that she said to me as if it was yesterday, possibly because they are also in one of my favourite hymns, 'Spirit of Life'.[1] If I had to sum up my theology, maybe I should just show people the words of the hymn: it would be a lot easier than trying to talk about it. I predict that those words are always going to be true for me, whereas I'm always changing my mind about the little things and so I wouldn't want to talk about those. And I guess for nurturing children then yes, it's roots and wings. What do you think, Josh?

Josh: My early memories of religious influence go back to trips to the Nightingale Centre, the Unitarian holiday centre in the Peak District. I was lucky enough to have contact with some of the great Unitarian characters of the late 1970s the 1980s. These visits made a deep and lasting impression on me, and they have had an effect on the way that I nurture my children as a Unitarian. The low-pressure but thought-provoking atmosphere that was created at Junior Weekends and Family Holiday Conferences appealed to my spiritual nature, despite my instinctive reservations about organised religion. On reflection, perhaps the encouragement that I received to 'find

---

1 Number 148 in *Sing Your Faith* (Lindsey Press, 2009).

my own way' has resulted in a tendency to fluctuate between infrequent and fairly regular Unitarian contact time, while always considering myself unquestioningly as Unitarian. Having been nurtured in a guided but open-minded way as a child, I would like to provide similar support to my children as they grow and develop.

Claire: Yes, we tend to nurture our children in the way that we were brought up, with the addition of all our adult life experiences. For us both, the travelling that we have done has reinforced the significance of nature-based religion in our lives. Throughout the world there are indigenous belief systems that are all surprisingly similar in their core elements. As well as this, we've both developed a better understanding of the main religions of the world and we hope to pass our knowledge and curiosity on to our children.

A sense of religious identity

Josh: So in nurturing our children as Unitarians we are focusing on giving them a sense of identity as Unitarians, but encouraging them to be confident to develop their own thoughts and beliefs. As well as this, we are hoping that they will grow up in a safe and stable family environment and be able to live a happy life in the wider world.

Claire: Yes, as I said – it's all about roots and wings! For growing the roots of a child's life, a naming ceremony seemed essential to us, even though it was more of a welcome to the world, as we had already named our daughter at the registry office. We decided to have the ceremony at home and to do it ourselves. This decision was influenced by circumstances at the time, by the people who were attending, and by the needs of our baby. The ceremony was unique, of course, bringing together our love of nature, family, and inclusivity. It included readings about family heritage, our hopes for her future, a Celtic blessing, and family poems. Messages were written on paper leaves, which were hung on a tree; relations who could not attend the ceremony wrote their messages and sent them beforehand. This was all incorporated into our baby's naming-day book, full of the special people in her life. The most obvious focus of the book is on family rather than on Unitarianism, but it does contain information about Unitarianism, about the churches attended in her first year, and a link to our support of the Nightingale Centre in her name. The tradition of recording such a ceremony in a book kept in a church has unfortunately been broken. We hope that the record in our baby's naming-day book demonstrates the importance that we ascribed to 'naming' her and welcoming her to the world. It was a firm root to start her off on her life.

The natural world

Josh: In our day-to-day lives, the significance of roots and wings is reflected also in our love of nature. We spend much of our leisure time in outdoor pursuits, so we are keen to incorporate this into the upbringing of our children. Exposing children to nature provides an enormous opportunity for development – in us, as well as our children! One of the joys of being with children is enjoying the fresh perspective that they bring to 'normal' experiences. A picnic becomes an exploration of buttercups and worms, instead of just a pleasant way to enjoy lunch. Nature provides a wonderful opportunity for learning. It comes naturally (pardon the pun!) to explain what we are seeing as we embark upon a walk. Trees, flowers, birds, animals, sights, sounds, and smells all become talking points. It is easy to convey a genuine feeling of wonder when encountering the natural world. We have enjoyed many walks, bike rides, swims, and camping holidays with our daughter. She also attends a weekly Nature Tots group which provides a lovely way for her to learn about and enjoy the natural world in the company of her friends. Once our son becomes old enough, he will be given the same opportunities, with the bonus of a big sister to show him what's what. Together we will all learn about respect and care for the natural world, and the traditions centred on events such as the solstices and other seasonal festivals. It will help our children to grow up, and us to stay young.

The weather can provide unexpected experiences which may have a significant impact on people of any age. I was reminded of this as an adult, when I attended a Khasi 'Waking' ceremony in north-east India while travelling in 2002. Khasi is a tribal religion with strong pagan elements, and I had expected to be spiritually moved by the Khasi fertility ceremony, but the aspect that I found most powerful on this day was the way in which the tribal leader dealt with a rainstorm. As the rain threatened to put an early end to the ceremony, the Khasi leader performed a ritual in the middle of the soggy field. He started chanting, then drew a circle in the mud and sprinkled some rice. He then proceeded to smash an egg dramatically in the middle of the circle as the chanting came to a crescendo. After a few moments of tension, the dark clouds rolled away, and the ceremony was able to continue. I was struck by the wonder of this event on many levels, and I hope that I am able to pass this kind of amazement on to my children. It was also a highly thought-provoking experience. Whether what I witnessed was coincidence or not, I felt a powerful connection to natural forces and I came away from the experience with a renewed respect for other people's cultures and beliefs. There are many things in this world that I do not understand, and I am happier to admit that than to express an opinion of which I am unsure. I consider this a good lesson to pass on to our children.

Social relationships

Claire: Of course, our children need confident wings to live happily in a world full of other children and adults. We aim for these to be inclusive wings too, just as our parents did. We encourage our two to spend lots of time with family and friends, younger and older. Every parent's challenge is to teach the social skills needed for successful relationships, and I guess we nurture children by modelling these skills as best as we can. It's certainly a learning curve, but we try to be inclusive and teach respect for others, even though our children are only small. We always try to think the best of people, and we hope to teach our children to do the same. The downside of this, of course, is that there is a lot to be scared of in the world, and we have to teach children to stay safe, as well as teaching them to be forgiving and empathetic.

We aim to teach our children to love and cherish all people in the wider world. There will be times when they will have to stand up for the rights of others in a climate of narrow-minded opinions. When we each reflect on our Unitarian upbringing, we remember times when our parents talked to us about gender stereotypes, sexuality, and religious and cultural backgrounds in a different way from the approach taken by the parents of a lot of our peers. A challenge to friends' negative comments on the first lesbian kiss on *Brookside* might explain why a few years later one of those friends first chose one of us to talk to about her sexuality. Believing that men and women are equal, and modelling the fact that either sex can achieve whatever they want, is also important, and we try to demonstrate this in day-to-day tasks and when talking with our children about ambitions.

Schooling

Claire: We value the chances for our children to have a broad religious education. The nearest primary school is a community school without any religious bias, and the nearest secondary school is linked to a church but doesn't have religious selection criteria. This is good for us, as it accords with our belief that children from all religions or none can be nurtured in education together, and everybody is included. We hope that both schools will teach about a variety of religions. It would be lovely if they knew what Unitarianism was, although from our experience it seems unlikely. ('I've never heard of it' was the only comment made by the RE teacher at my school.) Having said that, I must say that some church schools can provide valuable opportunities for spiritual development: an assembly in a Christian school where the majority of pupils are Muslim but all the pupils have a good knowledge of both faiths can be a wonderful ecumenical and spiritual experience. Assemblies in schools where all the pupils have the same religion must also be very meaningful for the people involved, but the unfortunate result of this, living where we do, is a strong element of segregation in some of our nearby schools. We would prefer an inclusive atmosphere in the schools that our children attend.

Church attendance

Josh: Aside from the choice of school, we intend to nurture the development of our children's own spiritual and religious beliefs by providing them with a range of opportunities to learn and consider some of the less tangible aspects of life. As a family we are likely to attend a Unitarian church on a fairly regular basis, as well as visiting the Nightingale Centre at Great Hucklow for several events each year. As our children grow older, we expect to involve them in the Unitarian youth programme, which benefited us both greatly at an age when we were formulating our conscious and sub-conscious beliefs.

Out in the world

Josh: Travel is a passion for both of us, and it also provides a great opportunity for exposure to a variety of religions and cultures. There is a huge appeal in using the informal context of 'being on holiday' as a vehicle for exploring the breadth of religious possibilities that exist. It is important to us that as well as hearing about alternative religions, our children will have first-hand experiences which will shape their thoughts and beliefs. For us it is as important to gaze into a camp fire or look up at the stars in order to stimulate our thoughts as it is to visit great cathedrals and temples in exotic countries. We hope to have many opportunities for all of these things and more before our children's wings enable them to fly the family nest.

In short, throughout our own childhoods, roots held us close and wings set us free. We hope that our children will experience the same, whatever they do, and wherever their lives take them.

Questions for discussion and reflection

1. How would you balance the exposition of your own personal views with providing a wider view of world religions to children?

2. How important is it for you that your children (or children in your family) follow the same faith as you in childhood – and in adulthood?

3. What are the advantages and disadvantages of regularly attending a place of worship in order to bring a child up in a particular faith?

4. What do you think about the use of Bible stories (and/or stories from other faiths) in order to teach children?

5. What role should schools play in developing the spiritual education of a child?

6. How should adults deal with the influence of TV and social media on the spiritual development of their children living in today's world?

7. Unitarians traditionally refrain from proselytising. How would you best create a balance between exposing children to Unitarian values, traditions, and customs and still encouraging them to explore other ideas and beliefs?

8. It is sometimes said that you cannot be born a Unitarian, you can only be born into a Unitarian family. You must come to Unitarianism as a conscious and thoughtful decision. What was your own journey into Unitarianism?

The authors

Claire and Josh Hewerdine live in Lancashire with their two small children. Josh is a business analyst in information technology, a keen runner and a huge cricket fan. Claire is a primary-school special-needs co-ordinator, and an enthusiast for music and the outdoors. Both grew up in Unitarian families. Josh was a member of Meadrow Unitarian Church. Claire was a member of an Anglican Sunday school and church choir until she was eight and then went on to attend West Kirby Free Church. They both attended the Unitarian Youth Programme and are now members of the Foy Society (www.ukunitarians.rg.uk/foy). Claire is also a member of the Unitarian Music Society (www.unitarianmusic.org.uk). Claire and Josh hope in the future to strengthen their links with their local chapels, to continue their support of the Nightingale Centre (www.thenightingalecentre.org. uk), and to raise their children as Unitarians.

Living sustainably
John Naish

Whenever someone mentions the word 'sustainable', a host of cosily positive images almost inevitably springs to mind: television's Tom and Barbara caper amiably in *The Good Life* while small children diligently tend junior vegetable patches and eco-warriors brave storm-wracked seas to defend whales from explosive harpoons.

Thus it is easy to see why a chapter on sustainable ways should feature in a book on spiritual living. It is so obvious (almost obligatory, in fact), that there might seem little point in reading further. But I do not come bearing tips on rainwater harvesting. There are far better sources for that elsewhere. I wish to be more soulfully challenging. I will argue that to live sustainably with spiritual integrity is no simple matter. It requires change from within as well as without. It begins from the centre of our being, and it must grow to embrace all the troubled expanses of our planet. In the process, it also requires that we reclaim the true meaning of the word 'sustainable', in all its indivisible dimensions.

Over the past few decades, the deep practice of sustainable living has been recycled into a lifestyle cliché. Its essential content has been hollowed out. While sustainable living is publicly lauded as a good thing, in reality it is practised mostly only sporadically, when it is not an inconvenience. Rather like vegetarians who enjoy a bacon sandwich, there is no shortage of people who believe that keeping a composting bin will amply offset the ozone depletion wrought by their next transatlantic holiday.

Indeed, we have come to the point where young people now often consider the S-word to be a turn-off, as they associate it with corporate PR people cynically 'greenwashing' products such as cars with spurious claims for their environmental benefits. Such greenwashing clearly works, however, or companies would not use it. The veneer that it creates may be thin to the point of transparency, but it salves the collective conscience.

Through processes such as this, the idea of sustainable living has become reduced to a mere add-on. In this respect, it has much in common with the popular, consumerist-driven idea that you can diminish spirituality into a convenient package: pick the easy bits – a few yoga poses and some sufi whirling – and it's job done, without any heavy lifting. But truly sustainable living inhabits the same postcode as true spiritual living: it lies at the core of daily existence. Therefore it requires that we examine the wellsprings of our deeds and habits.

Very often, ecological ideas are approached from the outside in. Books such as James Lovelock's *Gaia* series provide robust arguments for working to protect the planet, for the sake of ourselves and for future generations. But the spiritual approach to sustainable living comes from the inside out. This involves focusing primarily on something that I would call our individual 'spiritual ecology'. Through this, we can adopt habits of thought and action that sustain our inner selves and our physical bodies. At the same time, these actions contribute to the well-being of humanity and our ecosystem.

That's a big claim. But first, what do I mean by 'spiritual ecology'? Primarily, it is about living in a manner that enables us to sustain a soulful and reflective life in the midst of the harrying demands of the twenty-first century. These pressures are manifold. I think it is no coincidence that they constantly seem to conspire to push us from the spiritual path. Modern consumerism seems to be diametrically opposed to true spiritual living, which is branded as 'naff' – the converse of being rebelliously 'cool' – although I would argue that nowadays, if you want to be a properly rebellious individual, then you should go to church.

The most obvious pressure is materialistic. We are surrounded by propaganda, in the shape of advertising and media-shaped aspirations, that exhorts us to be dissatisfied with our current possessions and to dedicate our lives to the pursuit of greater material wealth. Such rampant acquisitiveness is in itself a threat to the environment, as it plunders ever more of the planet's finite resources before future generations can use them. But in spiritual terms, it brings two other threats of which we must be aware.

The first is that this materialism alienates us from the people around us, and ultimately from the global human community. Instead of recognising all humanity as a universal brother-sisterhood, to whom we bear crucial moral responsibilities, we are encouraged instead to see ourselves as unbonded, atomised consumers who must compete with neighbours and peers in public shows of shopping prowess.

Secondly, materialist pursuits rob us of a crucial resource for the spiritual life: time. Spirituality, in order to develop, needs time for contemplation, just as a young plant needs water. But busyness has become one of the great badges of pride in our consumer culture. 'Empty' time must be filled by getting, spending, and connecting. This emphasis on doing, rather than being, has created addictive patterns of behaviour across the population. Mobile phones are a case in point. Surveys increasingly show that people become anxious to the point of incapacity if they cannot access their phone, according to a report in *Psychology Today*.[1]

For the sake of our spiritual lives, we must strive to resist these pressures. I do not advocate living as hair-shirted hermits in tottering shacks. We all face the task, as individuals, of working out what compromises we must make between living spiritually and existing economically. Such balancing acts are at the heart of our spiritual ecology. But, with some effort, we may help ourselves to enter a benign cycle which helps to innure us to the spiritually toxic products of consumer society. To put it simply: less material acquisition can liberate more time, which can enable a greater sense of connection ... and in turn quash the temptation to block up our souls' spiritual yearnings with consumer bric-à-brac and junk infotainment. In this basic manner, if we look after our spiritual selves sustainably, we will also be helping the planet to look after itself. In the words of Mahatma Gandhi: 'Be the change you want to see in the world'.

So far, so good. But there is a price inherent in living like this. In nature, we have to sow in order to reap; and in order to take a spiritually sustainable life, we have to give a spiritually sustainable life to the cosmos. Otherwise, there is no synergy: we are simply dressing our rapacious ways in eco-friendly clothing. Therefore spiritual sustainability has to be an intrinsic part of a wider global duty. Our habits of spiritual ecology must feed into the global ecology. For no human is an island. Indeed, we depend for our daily

---

[1] 'Smartphone Addiction', 25 July 2013, by Dr Dale Archer.

survival on interconnection with the vast delicate interbeing of species and things that is essential to maintaining life on Earth.

In the wealthy West we have the best part of the deal, a life of apparent abundance and easy convenience. But it is balanced on the backs of millions of other human beings worldwide. Their collective carbon-footprint is not the size of a single toenail, compared with the galumphing consumption of the developed world. Nevertheless, these are the people whose farmlands and water supplies are among those worst afflicted by global climate change. These are also the people whose dreams and realities are destroyed by the profiteering ways of global corporations which bring cheap food and goods from across the globe on to our shelves.

To live mindfully, we must consume mindfully. To read in the *Ecologist Guide to Food*[2] of the shameful daily exploitation of pineapple farmers in Costa Rica and migrant banana growers in the Dominican Republic is a stark reminder that we should worry about more than air miles when buying food.

Moral obligations do not fade with distance. If we are to live spiritually, then we must nurture our global sense of personal integrity and interconnection. Here again, we see the intrinsic relationship between spiritual living and sustainable living. Our spiritual aims should raise our economic aims far higher than the short-term greed of shareholder profitability and boardroom rewards.

That higher aspiration has already been articulated: by the twentieth-century inventor and visionary, R. Buckminster Fuller. He declared that the aim of our global economic system should be *'To make the world work for 100 per cent of humanity in the shortest possible time through spontaneous cooperation without ecological offence or the disadvantage of anyone'*. Such lofty aims can nowadays seem depressingly unrealistic, given the fact that global levels of economic inequality and resource use are still rapidly increasing, rather than decreasing. It can feel hard sometimes to stay motivated. As individuals, we must hope that our spiritual lives can not only help us to live sustainably day by day, but also help to keep our higher aspirations at the heart of our ecological actions.

2   Andrew Walmsley, Leaping Hare Press, 2014.

Meanwhile, nature itself will never run short of wonders with which to inspire us. Did you know, for example, that forest trees talk with each other, trade nutrients between species, and actively foster their own young and the young of other trees? Suzanne Simard, a forest ecologist at the University of British Columbia, has discovered that forest trees organise themselves into networks, using an underground web of fungi that connects their roots. This 'wood-wide web', as some scientists have called it, enables trees to warn each other of insect attacks, and to deliver food and water to trees in need.

Simard's study shows how the oldest trees act as hubs, with up to 47 connections. She discovered how 'mother trees' use the network to feed shaded seedlings until they grow tall enough to reach the light. These mother trees can recognise their own direct offspring, and give them more nutrients. Simard also found that fir trees use the fungal web to trade nutrients with birch trees. The evergreens tide over the deciduous trees when they have sugars to spare, and they are repaid later that season. For the forest trees, the benefits of all this are better health, more photosynthesis, and greater resilience. Maybe they also get to gossip.

All that interconnection, interbeing, economic dealing, altruism, and even nepotism is happening beneath our feet. And it is happening in a deeply sustainable manner. Such marvels can surely inspire us to try to live likewise. As I have suggested earlier, the first step is to look after your own spiritual ecology and personal sustainability. In other words, look after yourself in a manner that balances production and consumption, and the rest may begin to follow.

Here are four basic suggestions that, from my own experience, can make a fundamental difference. No doubt you will have your own suggestions, too.

Grow some of your own food

It does not matter how little: it may be some salad rocket in a window box, not necessarily a vigorously tended allotment. Either can help to synchronise us with the seasons, as well as reminding us soulfully of the global effort required from people of all races and religions to bring food to our plates. (Not forgetting the bees, of course.)

Home-growing food also fosters deep appreciation of its preciousness. We are much less likely to wolf it, preferring instead to savour its flavours and textures. This mindful approach to food can, in turn, help to sustain our weight at healthy levels. Kathleen Melanson, a professor of nutrition at Rhode Island University, has found that when people eat more slowly, they consume significantly fewer calories. They enjoy their food more, feel fuller at the end of the meal, and still feel fuller an hour afterwards.

People who grow their own food develop a powerful aversion to throwing it out uneaten. In this country, about one third of the food bought from supermarkets is discarded. Home-grown food can prevent waste, helping to keep the domestic budget in balance, as well as conserving the world's resources.

Make 'empty' time

Consumer culture strives constantly to keep us economically engaged with entertainment, communications, shopping, and work. It denies us the crucial benefits of simply *being* rather than doing, of paying soulful attention to the world within us and without us. Brain-scans of non-religious Westerners who meditate for 20 minutes every day indicate increased development in cerebral regions associated with memory and attention. MRI scans at the Dalai Lama's monastery in Dharamsala, India, show that experienced meditators have much higher activity in their left prefrontal lobe, an area associated with positive states such as resilience, contentment, and optimism. This swamps activity in the right prefrontal lobe, which is linked with negative emotions such as fear and anxiety.

Meditation changes lives in another way. You can teach someone to meditate in ten minutes, but you can't teach them to keep meditating. That comes from within. Life has to change to accommodate it. With meditation, you have to dedicate a portion of each day to your own stillness. Our society might claim to be liberal and inclusive, but if you tell anyone (particularly in business), 'Sorry, not right now, this is my meditation time', you get suspicious looks. But if you shift your priorities in this direction, over time much deeper priorities may change, too.

Exercise

All exercise should take you somewhere, in a progress that may be internal as well as external. Exposing oneself to the chlorophyll cathedral that is nature can bring proven benefits to body and soul, an effect that is known scientifically as biophilia.

Exercise can tauten your spiritual fibres too. Some forms of yoga and tai chi, for example, are still rooted in the religious disciplines of their practice. Walking, running, and cycling can not only transport you physically but may also leave your mind free for meditation and reflection, and connect you to your community.

Going to the gym, however, may constitute mere exercise for the ego. The gyms themselves only use up energy, without creating any. Why they never attach the cycling machines to generators that can power hospitals remains a mystery to me. They represent a net waste of human energy and effort. Nature does not waste.

Practise gratitude

This can feel difficult, in the context of a culture which conspires to make us feel bad for not having enough stuff or for not being impressive enough. The antidote is simply to focus on what we do have, rather than what we don't. As well as enjoying historically unprecedented material riches, we also have the freedom to think and to worship how we choose. These basic rights are still denied to vast swathes of people across the globe.

In the words of the Reverend Dr. Michael Schuler, the parish minister of the First Unitarian Society of Madison: *'A sustainable future is conceivable and more probable if we can manage to instil in people a deeper sense of gratitude. In the final analysis, sustainability is as much a spiritual as a practical matter because it requires both a thorough reorientation of our relationship to the world and a radical revision of certain assumptions we have made about good and meaningful living.'*

Conclusion

I hope that the suggestions that I have offered will prove of some practical use in the daily challenge of maintaining a life that is sustainable spiritually and ecologically both for ourselves and for our planet. I shall close this chapter with another quote from Gandhi: *'As human beings, our greatness lies not so much in being able to remake the world – that is the myth of the atomic age – as in being able to remake ourselves.'*

Questions for reflection and discussion

1. Try ranking the following in your own order of priority (there is no 'right' answer here): *friendship, gratitude, empty time, spiritual practice, hobbies, working for others.* Perhaps you would like to add some other things to this list. Now, consider the ways in which consumer society prevents people from enjoying these experiences to the full.

2. How do you feel about your own 'spiritual ecology'? Do you feel that yours is in balance? Can you think of ways in which you could improve that balance? What factors, both practical and personal, might be hindering you from doing this?

3. Air travel is acknowledged to be the most environmentally damaging thing that people as individuals can do. But refusing to fly is considered by many people to be quite impossible. What rules for limiting air travel might you set yourself? (Perhaps you do already.) Could you set those same rules for others? And what spiritual foundations would you use for creating such rules?

4. Trying to balance your spiritual ecology can often make life inconvenient. Try reflecting on the most profound inconvenience that you have ever experienced in your life. (As an example, I think mine was looking after my mother at home while she was terminally ill.) What have your most profound personal inconveniences taught you and brought you?

Further reading

Frank, Thomas (1998) *The Conquest of Cool: Business Culture, Counterculture, and the Rise of Hip Consumerism,* University of Chicago Press.

Kumar, Satish (2014) *No Destination: Autobiography of a Pilgrim,* Green Books.

Schumacher, E. F. (1988) *Small is Beautiful: A Study of Economics as if People Mattered,* Abacus.

Seymour, John (1976) *The New Complete Book of Self-Sufficiency: The Classic Guide For Realists and Dreamers,* Dorling Kindersley.

The author

A very young John Naish was named as a Unitarian in 1968 at the church in New Road, Brighton. He is still a member and conducts weddings there. John's father had joined the faith as a result of his interest in world religions. (As a young man in the late 1930s, Naish Snr was the cook at the Shah Jahan mosque in Woking.)

John's adult life followed a similarly eclectic path. He worked as a bookie's boy and factory machinist, played in rock bands, and lived the long-haired biker life before he finally got a degree in English and Philosophy, travelled around the world, and stumbled into health journalism. He has written for all the Fleet Street broadsheets and spent 15 years in various editorial posts at *The Times*. He has written three books, including *Enough: Breaking Free From the World of More*. He is on the board of *The Inquirer*, the Unitarian newspaper. He now writes mainly for the *Daily Mail*.

John practises yoga and meditation, walks the Sussex Downs, restores old motorbikes and cars, and is often to be found pondering life on his allotment.

Living with loss
Sheila Bond

Several years ago, at a memorial service for a friend's husband, I heard for the first time a poem called 'The Dash' by Linda Ellis.[1] It makes the point that material things are unimportant, compared with how we live and love and how we spend the years of our life: 'the dash' between the year of our birth and the year of our death.

> *It matters not how much we own,*
> *the cars...the house...the cash.*
> *What matters is how we live and love*
> *and how we spend our dash.*

I found the words of this poem so inspiring that I kept a copy. Little did I think that I would be using it at the funeral of my own husband, David, some ten months later.

My experience of loss was sudden and, as far as I and my family were concerned, catastrophic. At the age of 54 my apparently healthy husband was out cycling with his friends one Sunday morning, when he collapsed, dead, from a massive heart attack. My children, aged 19 and 21, and I myself, were devastated.

Bereavement: the early stages

In the initial days and weeks after David's death, we experienced an outpouring of kindness: kindness from family, kindness from friends, kindness from casual acquaintances and even from complete strangers. My daughter told me that from the moment when she arrived home on

---

1 http://www.linda-ellis.com/the-dash-the-dash-poem-by-linda-ellis-.html.

that most shocking day her overriding impression was of kindness. Food appeared on our doorstep as if from nowhere – I remember casseroles and rhubarb crumbles among many other offerings – so useful, as providing family meals was very low on my own list of priorities. I have no doubt that it was this kindness that got us through that first period of intense grief.

Initially it was hard for me to accept some of this kindness. I had thought of myself as a self-contained and independent person. I had never wanted to be indebted to others. But I gradually came to realise that the offers of help were very genuinely meant. Practical help was something concrete that friends could do to help us in our distress. So I gratefully accepted, and help it did. Friends phoned regularly. I often wondered whether my close friends had some kind of rota: it seemed that most nights I would have a call from one or other of my friends, just to see how things were. Or I would be invited round to someone's house for a meal, or out for a coffee. I really looked forward to these events, even if I found them hard when they arrived. Strangely, if no one phoned me it did not occur to me that I could phone them. I would not have known how to start the conversation. I would not have wanted to admit to anyone that I was phoning because I felt lonely. For many months I just let myself be carried along, without too much thought about where I was heading.

Friends invited me to the village pub quiz. I didn't want to go and I didn't enjoy it. However, at that particular time I felt as if I would never enjoy anything, ever, again. I remember feeling so miserable after that first quiz that I took myself out for a walk as soon as I got home. Walking, in the middle of the night, not really knowing where I was going or why. Panicking when my torch battery went flat and I could not find the path that I needed to get home. Stumbling into thicker undergrowth and wondering if I would have to stay out until dawn. Once I had finally found my way home, feeling rather ashamed of myself that I had been so foolhardy. Realising that I needed to be more sensible for the sake of my family, who still needed me. Persevering with the pub quiz because I didn't want to let my friends down: after all, they were doing their best to help me. And gradually, over the months, despite myself, and thanks to the unfailing kindness of all my friends, being aware that sometimes I had actually enjoyed myself.

Bereavement: the next stage

But after recovering from the initial period of shock, I was plagued with questions such as 'Why am I here?', 'What is the point?', and 'What now?' I worked full-time as a physiotherapist and kept a menagerie of animals which comprised two dogs, two cats, some ducks, and a horse. This meant that keeping busy during the week was not a problem – it was more a case of finding enough hours in the day to do everything that needed to be done. But I remember that in those early weeks the relief of getting to the end of the week was closely followed by a dull realisation that there was now a whole weekend to fill. In my search for meaning, I visited many churches, of different denominations, near and far. Although I met many kind and lovely people, I did not feel spiritually at home anywhere. I felt that I was sitting on the fringe wherever I visited – wanting to be part of a community but unable to sign up to all the rules.

I had been brought up in the United Reformed Church and had attended weekly services and Sunday School until my mid-teenage years. I drifted away from my church at around the time it was hoped that I would make the commitment to be confirmed and join the church: I just did not feel able to make that statement of belief. For the next 30 years religion played very little part in my life, except for a brief spell when my children were young and I took them to my local Congregational chapel.

It was during my struggle to rebuild my life after David's death and find some meaning from my loss that I discovered Unitarianism. In the evenings, late at night, I searched the internet. One night I came across the Progressive Christianity Network[2] and read on with great interest. This was better. It sounded more like me – this was a group of people who acknowledged that they didn't have all the answers but invited exploration and discussion. It was at one of their monthly meetings that I overheard one of their members talking about the Unitarians. She said that she had been to a Unitarian service in Oxford, and thought she would go again. I had not heard of Unitarians, so went home and promptly looked them up.

2 www.pcnbritain.org.uk.

I was immediately attracted by the words on the website: 'Unitarianism is an approach based not on dogma, but on reason' and 'Unitarianism encourages individual freedom, equality for all and rational thought. There is no list of things that Unitarians must believe: instead we think that everyone has the right to reach their own conclusions.'

My nearest Unitarian chapel was in Oxford, further than ideal from my home near Newbury, but I set off the following Sunday to investigate. After that first service, my initial thought was: 'Where have the Unitarians been all my life, and why didn't I find them before?' Here at last was a faith that I could relate to. I well remember those first few months: every service had a different leader, with new ideas which would send me rushing home to explore their thoughts in more depth. I read with great interest; in fact at one stage it seemed that each week I added another title to the list of books that I wanted to explore. The subsequent reading filled the empty hours late at night when I sometimes found it difficult to sleep. I started to attend Chapel regularly and enjoyed it from the outset. I found that the discipline of attending a weekly service gave my weekend some much-needed structure, and I started to look forward to Sundays. As well as the readings and the address, I found the words of the prayers and hymns comforting. In addition, I was introduced to a friendly community of like-minded people. Although it was challenging to get to know another group of strangers, in many ways it felt right. The Unitarians in Oxford were very important to me in those early years, between the initial shock and the gradual rebuilding of my life. I think they gave me hope – hope that I could find some sort of meaning for that 'Dash', mentioned at the start of this chapter, that I had been so determined to fill meaningfully, but not sure how.

In my visits to other churches, I had been hoping to find a belief system that I could accept, especially an idea of God. I felt that without this it was hard for me to find a purpose for what was left of my 'Dash'. When I read that some Unitarians believed in God and some didn't, and that there could be many different pathways to God, I felt encouraged. I found a definition of God that felt real to me: God is 'what I believe to be of supreme worth', and the word can perhaps represent qualities and ways of living to be found deep within myself and others. I realised that what I had been looking for initially perhaps does not exist for me; while in my initial stages of bereavement that thought had seemed unbearable, but the Unitarian faith gave me hope and even confidence that life could still be meaningful, enriching, and spiritual.

Cliff Reed, in his booklet *Unitarian: What's That?*, articulates some of the ideas that I had found in the poem by Linda Ellis, and I found his words very helpful:

> Unitarians take the view that, in any case, the focus of our attention should be this world. Our concern is better directed to considering how we should live our lives in the here and now. A life well lived is the best preparation for death, whatever may lie beyond it.[3]

Another Unitarian writer who inspired me was Forrest Church. I found a lot of wisdom in his book *Love and Death: My Journey through the Valley of the Shadow*.[4] One sentence that particularly inspired me was this: 'The one thing that can't be taken away from us, even by death, is the love we give away before we go.'

I was also attracted to the concept of Mindfulness, or being fully aware of the present moment, and was interested to hear many references to it in Unitarian services. The following ideas struck a strong chord with me:

> It is a challenge to live *mindfully*: the practice of living fully in the moment, or the 'eternal now'. In part, true mindfulness can be achieved only by dispelling illusions – and some of the most compelling illusions are those that we inherit from the past. The Unitarian movement's traditional dedication to sound historical scholarship is the chief way in which we have sought to uncover the truth about the past, in order that we may live ever more in the moment, free from illusion, but still open to the many eternal truths which history has preserved for us.[5]

3   Cliff Reed, *Unitarian: What's That?* (Lindsey Press, 1999).
4   Boston: Beacon Press, 2008.
5   Andrew Brown, 'Is There a Future for the Unitarian Christian Tradition?' in *Prospects for the Unitarian Movement*, ed. Matthew F. Smith (Lindsey Press, 2002), p. 9.

One (non-Unitarian) book that was very helpful to me at this stage was Hugo Gryn's *Chasing Shadows*,[6] about his experiences in the Holocaust and of finding God in Auschwitz. He came to an understanding of what God meant to him quite suddenly, in a time of terrible personal suffering. I still aspire to deepen my understanding of the meaning of God, but Hugo Gryn's experiences and those shared by other Unitarian writers led me to accept that it is likely to be a gradual process.

In the Oxford chapel I took part in discussion groups which met over lunch after Sunday services. These groups helped me to understand more of the Unitarian perspective on some of life's big questions. I was able to explore my own thoughts within a supportive group, and I found this both interesting and helpful, if challenging at times. Other group members shared some of their own life experiences, and I was humbled to hear the stories of others' difficulties. I valued the openness to other opinions and acceptance of different ideas that are typical of Unitarian values.

Bereavement: moving on

Away from the Sunday service, I felt a strong need to do something that I felt to be worthwhile with my spare time. I trained as a volunteer with the charity Action for Children and became a mentor for a young person who had just left the care system and was starting to live independently. I met up with him monthly for a period of two years, and we shared some memorable outings, including my first attendance at a football match and his first visit to a pizza restaurant. I think I enjoyed the trips almost as much as he did!

Gradually the grief lessened and now, five years after David's death, I think very differently from the first or even the second year after my loss. I feel confident that I can go forward and do something worthwhile in that 'Dash' mentioned in the first paragraph. Because we none of us know how long our Dash will be, I try to be aware of every moment as it happens

6 Penguin Books, 2001.

and to live each day as fully as possible. Because I don't want to waste those moments, I don't feel under pressure to do things simply because they are expected of me. Deep within me I think there may always be a sadness, but that no longer distresses me. This state of mind is beautifully expressed in the words of one of my favourite hymns, *Flying Free*, by Don Besig.[7] It acknowledges that 'life is not a distant sky without a cloud' and confronts the inevitable truth that 'all too soon we've lost the day'; but finally it affirms that, despite everything, 'life has taught me how to fly'.

Questions for discussion and reflection

1. In what way do your beliefs about what happens after death affect how you react to death?
2. How can you best help a person after the loss of someone close to them?
3. What do you think Forrest Church means by 'The one thing that can't be taken away from us, even by death, is the love we give away before we go'?
4. How can we use the past, with particular reference to Unitarian history, to help us to live more in the present moment?
5. Which words inspire you to find more meaning for your life?

The author

Sheila has lived in Berkshire since 1993. She has two grown-up children. Her husband, David, died in 2010. Sheila is a Chartered Physiotherapist and worked in the NHS for 30 years. She left in 2014 to complete her training as a teacher of Mindfulness. She has been a Unitarian since 2012 and belongs to the Chapel Society of Manchester College, Oxford, whose services she attends regularly (www.ukunitarians.org.uk/oxford). She recently led a service of worship there for the first time.

Sheila volunteers for Action for Children as a mentor and advocate for children in the care system. She loves animals and the countryside. In her spare time she enjoys long walks with her border collie, Fizz, whom she trains for the sport of Agility. Her favourite way to explore the countryside is on horseback.

---

7   Number 167 in *Sing Your Faith*, Lindsey Press, 2009.

Part 2: Making Waves and Lighting Fires

Working for justice
Bob Pounder

When I received my union card as a member of the Fire Brigades Union in 1979, it was a significant moment. My decision to join the union was not the result of some persuasive recruitment process, nor prompted by the fact that all my mates at the firefighters' training school were joining. No, I joined because I wanted to. Ten years previously, at the age of 15, I had joined the Royal Navy, and that had been my working life up until this point. There were no union rights in the Navy, and if you were told to jump, the only question you could ask was 'How high?'. Nevertheless, in spite of this militarisation, I was becoming more politically aware and found common ground with a friend of mine; together (albeit from a distance) we followed the developments of the famous two-year Grunwick strike, led by Asian women from 1976 to 1978. A more immediate trigger was the firefighters' first national strike, which began in November 1977 and lasted for nine weeks. By that time I was a naval firefighter, working on the fire station at Royal Naval Air Station Culdrose in Cornwall. I felt, as many others did, that if the firefighters who were uniformed and disciplined could wield union power, then it was time that we in the Royal Navy should follow suit. In other words, I was inspired by the working-class militancy of the 1970s and hoped that it would lead to a more democratic and socialist society.

But two years later the Thatcher government came to power, and even before that there were clouds on the horizon that I could not foresee at the time. I little realised how hard it could be not only to struggle against the employers and the management but also to struggle with your own people in the battle of ideas. I discovered that many of the trade-union officials I met and worked with, with honourable exceptions, were often worse than useless. Nevertheless, I never gave up, and on a long journey the Labour Party, the Militant Tendency, the Revolutionary Communist Party, and finally the Workers Revolutionary Party became my world and my university. My mentor for many years was Dave Hallsworth, a dear friend and comrade. Dave was a generation older than me. A committed socialist, he spent time in prison before being chucked out of the Royal Navy in the 1950s for being a member of the Communist Party of Great Britain. Disillusioned by the events of 1956 and the crushing of the Hungarian uprising, he later left the party, but remained a class fighter all of his life. I learned a great deal from him.

Indeed, I owe a debt of gratitude to the labour and trade-union movement, because my involvement as a union activist, mainly with the Fire Brigades Union and later with the National Union of Journalists and the Faithworkers branch of Unite, has provided me with a certain insight and experience. And the fact remains that, in spite of everything, you are still better off being in a union than outside it.

I know from experience that trade unions are far from perfect, that they often fail to measure up to the expectations of the individual member, and also that in wider disputes some union leaders can be self-serving and cowardly. Combative trade unionists and workers often find themselves in conflict with this self-interested bureaucracy. I know: I've been there myself. But positive experiences of battles fought with and for union members against management injustice have far outnumbered these disappointments. Some of the injustices that members have faced have been appalling, and the kinds of story that I have heard and sometimes been part of never seem to get the media publicity that they deserve.

Trade-union rights are human rights. People sometimes talk about rights as if they fall ready-made from the sky, or as if they are simply handed out by benevolent governments and employers. They are not. Rights have to be fought for, and once they are obtained we have to struggle to hold on to them. It is a sad fact of life that unions ever had to exist at all. They came into existence only because of the social, political, and economic injustice that comes from a society based on the haves and have-nots.

First encounter with Unitarianism

When, in 1993, I first stepped into a Unitarian church, it was a return to religion – but not the religion of my childhood: the dogmatic certainties of the evangelical Christianity that I had experienced with the Salvation

Army. I am still very fond of the Salvation Army. I like its exuberance, the brass bands, the 'Blood and Fire' insignia, and the passion and the sincerity of many of its soldiers and preachers. But I knew that underneath all that there was a steely dogma, an assured certainty that the Bible was the literal word of God, every word regarded as indisputably true. As a boy and as a recruit to the band, I was told, 'Don't keep asking questions. You'll never learn anything if you keep asking questions.' There was love and energy in the Salvation Army, but also a sort of conservatism. I could not accept the theology, and that is why I could not go back.

As I walked into the Unitarian Church at Mossley, Edith Barber greeted me at the front door. She said, 'A stranger!', and I replied 'Well, it says outside, *Everybody Welcome*, so I'm here'. Edith handed me a red hymnbook. The words on the front cover read *Hymns of Faith and Freedom*, which seemed to express everything that I was looking for: *faith* and *freedom*, freedom to think and to be allowed to do so within the church. I liked the chalice logo too; it seemed a good symbol, almost like an oil lamp that one might read about in the Bible stories. But although the chalice has become a symbol of our denomination, from my Unitarian Christian point of view it cannot replace the cross, that symbol of the church universal, that symbol of sacrificial love.

From the church at Mossley, and its Minister the Revd. Pat Shaw, I began to get a feel for the denomination and to understand something of its history and its special theology. The congregation were warm and friendly, but it was a bit hard in those days to square my revolutionary left politics and militant trade unionism with sitting down on a Sunday morning with a predominantly female congregation, many already in their late seventies and eighties.

In 1997 I was elected to the position of Brigade Secretary of the Fire Brigades Union in Greater Manchester. This job became so all-consuming that I had curtailed all Unitarian activities by 1998, and what little time I had left was spent on the Workers Revolutionary Party. But throughout the years that followed, I continued in some way to acknowledge the spiritual side of my life. In 2004 I retired from the fire service, but not entirely in circumstances that I would have wanted. There had been a disastrous national strike in 2002, and a leadership collapse at national level which led to demoralisation and reaction. Time to go – after 25 years in the fire service, 18 years as an operational firefighter and what you could say were seven tumultuous years as a full-time union secretary.

Re-engaging with Unitarianism

It was not long before I found my second Unitarian church, Oldham Unitarian Chapel, in 2005. With the freedom of retirement and tenuous self-employment, I became more involved with the life of the church once again. As the years have passed, my views and my life have changed. Theologically, I have been greatly influenced by the work of the Unitarian minister Revd. Dr. David Doel, a man whom I deeply admire and whose work and ministry confirmed to me religion's deepest truth: the power of love. This truth first became more accessible to me through his wonderful work on the interface of depth psychology and religion. Through David's work, my Christian faith, the faith of my childhood, was made mature, resilient, and deep. I owe him a great debt. In 2010 I trained as a minister and was appointed to serve the Unitarian congregation in Oldham, which is a great privilege.

As I embraced Unitarianism and then grew more deeply involved with the Christian faith, I came to realise that Marxism did not really offer the systemic solution that I had originally believed. To put it bluntly, I abandoned ideology – not just Marxism, but all ideologies. I came to see them as a trap that can lead us unwittingly to positions where the end justifies the means, and the kind of thinking that can create concentration camps, labour camps, summary executions, pointless terrorism, and the horrors of war: man's inhumanity to man.

I have always been haunted by Storm Jameson's words in the introduction to *The Diary of Anne Frank*, where she questions what it is that moves people to feel such contempt for others that they can come to see a Jew or a political opponent as vermin to be stamped out. She ascribes this evil to a doctrine which men can 'press over their ears and eyes' and thus become impervious to the cries of the victims of torture in their agony. She shows how human reason can be employed to justify any cruelty, by showing that it is essential to some grand majestic plan. In other words, no matter how noble or ignoble the cause, or how extreme the violence we may use, history tells us that there is no simple solution to the perceived injustices of this world. By that I don't mean that there is not a solution: just that injustice cannot be permanently resolved through guns and bombs and prison camps. But I do hope and believe that it can be done in other, more realistic, ways.

Combining religion and politics

To its credit, the General Assembly of Unitarian & Free Christian Churches gives *de facto* recognition to the role of trade unions in its relations between ministers and congregational committees. This makes possible the resolution of conflicts and disagreements through agreed procedures such as grievance and disciplinary processes, taking into account employment law and the tenets of natural justice. As a representative for the Faithworkers branch of Unite, I have witnessed the intransigence of other denominations in refusing to accept or recognise trade-union representation. In 2014 I visited the offices of the north-west synod of another denomination to represent one of its ministers. Before the meeting had even started, I was informed that, since ministers are office holders rather than employees, the Employment Relations Act did not apply: in other words, that ministers were considered a special case and not entitled to the same employment protection as other workers. I pointed out that as Christians we are called to apply the highest standards of justice, and that the principles of natural justice still underpin the law of the land. In this case the matter was eventually resolved satisfactorily.

A less happy outcome followed a few months later, when I became involved with a case involving a disabled woman, a student at a theological college in the north of England. The student, who was a Unite member, was expelled from the college – but the grounds for the dismissal were never stated clearly, certainly not to the individual or to her union representatives. The college principal was not open to attempts at informal resolution by the union. I even asked for an inquiry into the matter, but to no avail. No appeal against the student's expulsion was allowed. Certainly, the college was acting within the law, but there I saw no justice or compassion. The struggle goes on, but some Christians, it seems, need to be reminded of St Paul's injunction that the letter of the law kills, but the spirit brings life.

Robert Sheldon, for many years the MP for Ashton-under-Lyne, once told me that in order to bring change you have to convince others; a simple statement, but a profound truth. The only way to win trade-union disputes is to win the hearts and minds of others in big numbers, to achieve critical mass; you must be prepared to escalate. In the words of Dave Hallsworth, 'The only way to win a dispute is to step it up'. This in my mind is basic trade unionism. In his song *Talking Union Blues*, Pete Seeger sums it up:

> The boss won't listen when one man squawks,
> but he's got to listen when the union talks.
> He looks out of his window and what does he see?
> But a thousand pickets and they all agree
> he's a bastard – unfair slave-driver,
> bet he beats his own wife!

Convincing people, winning both hearts and minds, is the only sustainable solution. As Che Guevara is supposed to have said, 'Solidarity is the love of the people'. This solidarity, this love, is the only guarantee of any future for humanity; but we need to see love in action. In a very real but radical sense, this love is already alive and present in the world. If it wasn't, the world would not exist. But this is a fact rarely acknowledged. I like to think that we get an echo of this in the first chapter of that most beautiful of the Christian gospels, the Gospel of John: 'The light [love] shines in the darkness, but the darkness can never extinguish it.'

It's like John Lennon's famous Christmas song, *War is Over (If You Want It)*. The Kingdom of God is here right now: we only have to reach out and take it. The Kingdom of God is peace and joy in the Holy Spirit. Lennon's song is not merely 'pacifist' – it is revolutionary! And when we look back again to the Gospel of John, we read that this light that comes into the world is not recognised, and that even among his own people he is rejected. The unpalatable truth is, as John says, a preference for the darkness. The light shines in the darkness and exposes the truth about ourselves, the selfishness, the greed, the fear; our vulnerability, our insecurities, our egoistic individualism. And we can't have that, so we want to close the light down. We want to feel OK about ourselves and we don't want to be reminded about our shortcomings; instead we want the approval of the world. So the light is rejected, and an opportunity for growth and liberation is lost, because we fear the light; we fear the truth because the ego fears its own annihilation. Christ was crucified because the truth of his message was unbearable to the world: unbridled love is a threat to the status quo.

There is division in the world – that is part of our everyday reality – but problems arise not just when we are caught up in the divisions but because we also help to perpetuate them, often quite unawares. Jesus taught that a kingdom divided against itself cannot stand, nor even a house. The demons of division are represented in the story of the man from the Gadarene: his demons are named 'Legion, for we are many'. Real strength and wholeness lies in unity. In trade-union mythology the workers are united, standing together in their collective struggle.

For years I used to hear that same old refrain: 'The unions have too much power'. Well we can't say that today in 2016, as young people – if they can find work at all – are terribly exploited; the low-wage economy is the norm, and the growth of the zero-hours contract as a form of tenuous hand-to-mouth living continues apace. Increasing levels of homelessness and poverty are becoming ever more apparent, as 'benefits sanctions' and cuts to social spending slice ever deeper. It is not political spin or manifestos that are needed today, but the emergence of the prophetic voice calling us to the greatest of all laws: to love God and to love our neighbour as ourselves. To be responsible for the least of those among us, to bring God's Kingdom to earth, to become who we really are, and to make love a way of life.

Questions for discussion and reflection

1. The rulebook of the Fire Brigades Union states the union's immediate
   aims as 'to serve its members by winning for them the best possible
   conditions, and to serve the community by encouraging its members to be
   skilled at their craft. ... The Fire Brigades Union recognises that workers,
   however employed, can only improve their lot by their own endeavours
   and organisation. A richer and fuller life can be achieved only by similar
   means.' *Within the context of the above statement, give examples of your idea
   of a 'richer and fuller life'.*

2. Dr Martin Luther King once said, 'Whenever you are engaged in work that
   serves humanity and is for the building of humanity, it has dignity and
   it has worth.' Work should serve to give each person a sense of identity,
   because more often than not we are defined by our occupation. Through
   our employment we participate directly in the world and serve the needs of
   others. The work that we do should therefore have a spiritual dimension,
   because under the right conditions it should be a source of pride and
   joy. In serving others in this way, we are serving God and we are serving
   ourselves. *Thinking about the spirituality of work, what aspect of your job/
   occupation gives you most joy?*

3. Class consciousness is a waking up to certain political realities like the
   rallying cry of the Peasants' Revolt in 1381: 'When Adam delved and Eve
   span, who was then the gentleman?', recalling the primitive communism
   of a bygone age. But we have to go further for the revolution, as John
   Lennon understood. There has to be a revolution of the heart. The full
   awakening is expressed in the words of Jesus in the Sermon on the Mount,
   the central tenets of the Christian faith giving witness to the power of love.
   *Do you agree or disagree with the idea that the Sermon on the Mount points
   to a true awakening? Give your reasons. Is the power of love enough to change
   the world?*

Further reading

Doel, David (2009) *The Man They Called The Christ*, Unitarian Christian Association.

Funk, Mary Margaret (1999) *A Mind at Peace: Spiritual Disciples of John Cassian and the Desert Fathers*, Lion Books.

Kempis, Thomas à (c. 1420) *The Imitation of Christ*.

King, Martin Luther (1963) *Strength to Love,* Harper & Row.

Merton, Thomas (1949) *New Seeds of Contemplation* (reprinted 2007 by New Directions Publishing Corporation).

Sillitoe, Alan (1959) *The Loneliness of the Long Distance Runner and Other Stories,* W.H. Allen.

Tolle, Eckhart (1999) *The Power of Now*, New World Library.

Trotsky, Leon (1930) *My Life: An Attempt at an Autobiography.*

About the author

Bob Pounder joined the Royal Navy at the age of 15 years in 1969, at the boys' training establishment, HMS Ganges, Ipswich. He served for 10 years in the Navy before joining the fire service in 1979. Following seven years' service as a full-time official in the Fire Brigades Union, he joined the Manchester branch of the National Union of Journalists as a freelance writer, eventually becoming a union representative for the NUJ and a campaigner for asylum seekers. Since 2010 he has been the Minister of the Unitarian congregation in Oldham, Lancashire.

Bob writes: 'As I look back over my life, I give thanks for all those people who have in one way or another helped me to become, in spite of my many faults, who I am today. In my many years' service as a union rep, I had the privilege of helping so many people in so many different ways. I think this was in itself a ministry of sorts, as authentic as anything that I might do today.'

Taking our values to work
Peter Hawkins

The morality we have lived by was fragmentary only. We must abandon it in favour of the complete, all-embracing love expressed in 'reverence for all life'.
(Albert Schweitzer[1])

These [current] situations have caused Sister Earth, along with all the abandoned of our world, to cry out, pleading that we take another course. Never have we so hurt and mistreated our common home as we have in the last two hundred years. The problem is that we still lack the culture needed to confront this crisis. We lack leadership capable of striking out on new paths and meeting the needs of the present with concern for all and without prejudice towards coming generations.
(Pope Francis, 'Laudato Si: On Care for Our Common Home', 2015[2])

On a Sunday, it is very possible for me to attend a Unitarian service, or spend time meditating, and feel open and reflective, accepting of others, calm and present. If I have managed to find time to work in our walled garden, I find that my positive sense of well-being is even greater and more embodied.

But then comes Monday. For me this sometimes means a commute to London ... train delays, while I try to juggle e-mails and mobile-phone calls ... then the hassle of crowded tube trains, and arriving late for important meetings with other cross and irritated people. Transport, however, is only one factor producing stress and anxiety. Many of the people I work with are coping with enormous job pressures, living with daunting uncertainty, and facing challenges for which there is no easy road map.

1   http://www.schweitzerfellowship.org/about/albert-schweitzer/quotes-by-albert-schweitzer/ (accessed July 2015).
2   http://www.catholicherald.co.uk/news/2015/06/18/full-text-laudato-si/

It is so much easier to be spiritual and good natured in periods of reflection than it is in the heat of frantic action. So I have become increasingly interested in spiritual practices for the frenetic and hectic moments of our working life. Part of my professional life involves helping large organisations to explore their purpose, vision, strategy, and core values. Yet many organisations do this in a way that ends up as well-crafted words, stuck on the office wall, which have little impact on how life is actually lived, or how work is carried out. Worse still, such a process can lead to increased cynicism, as the rift grows between the rhetoric of the value statements and the reality of everyday behaviour. So I have become increasingly interested in how we can take our values to work, and make our values work at work.

Developing our values and moral code

In the Judeo-Christian tradition, the Old Testament presented a moral code based on rules forbidding what was perceived as morally wrong. This is most clearly exemplified in the Ten Commandments, each beginning: 'You shall not ...'. Jesus emphasised a new moral sensibility that was more positively expressed in terms of what we *should* do. His moral teachings, rather than focusing exclusively on individual behaviour, could be described as *relational*:

> One of the teachers of the law asked Jesus, 'Of all the commandments, which is the most important?' 'The most important one,' answered Jesus, is this: "Hear, O Israel: The Lord our God, the Lord is one. Love the Lord your God with all your heart and with all your soul and with all your mind and with all your strength." The second is this: "Love your neighbour as yourself." There is no commandment greater than these.'
> (Mark 12: 28–31)

Jesus also insisted that morality was not just about behaviour but also about our thoughts and intentions:

You have heard that it was said to the people long ago, 'Do not murder', and 'Anyone who murders will be subject to judgment'. But I tell you that anyone who is angry with his brother will be subject to judgment...You have heard that it was said, 'Do not commit adultery'. But I tell you that anyone who looks at a woman lustfully has already committed adultery with her in his heart.
(Matthew 5: 21–22, 27–28)

Unitarianism developed from the Judeo-Christian tradition, but with a much greater emphasis on a personal morality informed by individual conscience, encouraging individuals to find their own values and make informed moral choices. The traditional Unitarian toast celebrated 'Freedom, Reason, and Tolerance'. Danny Crosby, a current Unitarian minister, has provided a useful contemporary version of this traditional trinity of values, interpreting Freedom as taking personal authority and responsibility, Respect as the celebration of difference, and Tolerance as openness to other views.[3] We need to build on the Unitarian encouragement to be guided by our own individual conscience and find our own internal moral compass. Learning as a young adult to develop one's inner conscience and ethical values is critically important, particularly these days, when so many young people are vulnerable to grooming and brainwashing via the internet, smart phone, and peer pressure.

But I think we need to go further. I have written elsewhere[4] about the problems that arise from adopting an exclusively individualistic religion and moral code, and about the need to develop one's values and morality in dialogue with others.[5] Individually we are all capable of 'wilful blindness' (Heffernan 2011) and illusion, delusion, and collusion, so as well as taking our values to work, we constantly need to learn at work how to evolve our values and grow our ethical maturity. I am acutely aware how hard it is to step back and see my own actions and their unintended consequences, and how easy it is for me to fall into wilful blindness concerning my own

3   Danny Crosby, 'From Nothing to Everything', *The Inquirer*, 20 June 2015.
4   Hawkins 1999, 2006a.
5   Hawkins 2006b.

behaviour and its consequences. I believe that we all need reflective spaces where we can stand back and look at our work and be challenged by critical friends on what we have done and how we can do it more effectively. This is why I have spent so much of my life developing, practising, teaching, and writing about supervision and reflective practice as an essential practice for all professionals who work in depth with other people, be they doctors, psychologists, counsellors, psychotherapists, coaches, ministers, social workers, teachers, or nurses. We need a place where we not only reflect on our own work but where we can contract with a colleague to challenge our shadow side, our blind spots, deaf spots, and dumb spots, and our use and misuse of power. All supervision is fundamentally concerned with growing our ethical maturity, which Carroll[6] defines as: 'having the reflective, rational and emotional capacity to decide what actions are right and/or wrong, having the courage to do it and being publicly accountable for my decision'.

Evolving our values and moral code

We need to move beyond the goal of defining our own values and ethical beliefs. If we fail to progress beyond that first essential step, we are in danger of becoming self-righteous, imprisoned by our own myopia. To quote Hazrat Inayat Khan, the great Sufi Universalist teacher (1882–1927):

> The less wisdom one has, the more one holds to one's ideas. In the wisest person there is the willingness to submit to others. And the most foolish person is always ready to stand firm to support his own ideas.

He wrote about how the spiritually mature always see any issue from at least two perspectives, their own and that of the other. All adults, not only those in the caring professions, need dialogical challenge, and I have

---

6   Michael Carroll (1996) *Counselling Supervision: Theory, Skills and Practice.* London, UK: Cassells.

written elsewhere[7] about how we could build dialogical processes into Unitarian religious practice. In my contribution to a collection of essays entitled *Being Together: Unitarians Celebrate Congregational Life*, I wrote about the need to move beyond dialogue to *trialogue*, a spiritual practice which I defined as follows:

> A dialogue that not only involves two or more people but also involves listening and attending to the sacred that emerges from beyond the personal and inter-personal domains. Creating the space for grace.

Evolving from human-centric to eco-centric values

According to the spiritual teacher Krishnamurti (1895–1996), although we may think we are thinking our own thoughts, we are often thinking our culture's thoughts. One critical way in which our culture thinks through us is that our beliefs and morality formed by the Judeo-Christian and Unitarian traditions are very human-centric. We now urgently need an ethical foundation that goes further than this. We need an eco-spiritual ethic which recognises that the whole human economy is a wholly owned subsidiary of Earth's biosphere – and unless we wake up to this fact, our whole human economy will be shut down.

I once fell into the error of talking to my good friend Professor Peter Reason, while sitting in his garden, about organisations that create value. 'Rubbish!' was his explosive retort: 'The only thing that creates value on this earth is that' – pointing to the brilliant burning sun, the source of light, warmth, photosynthesis and all the things that make life possible on this planet. 'We humans don't create value', he added. 'We just appropriate it and move it around.'

There is currently an important sea change taking place in thinking and writing about value creation. Michael Porter, one of the most successful

7   Hawkins 2006b.

49

strategy writers of the late twentieth century, wrote a key paper with Mark Kramer on how we need to move from focusing on 'shareholder value' to focusing on 'shared values' for all stakeholders. They point out that if an organisation is not creating benefit for all its stakeholders, it is not building its own long-term sustainability.[8]

I have argued that the stakeholders for whom an organisation must create on-going benefit include customers, partners and suppliers, employees, investors, the communities in which the organisation operates, and the more-than-human world.[9] But the more-than-human world is of a different order from the other stakeholders, for the organisation's activity is entirely dependent upon it, and it is the context within which everything else takes place.

So how do I try to get my values to work?

I propose four steps that I consciously try to practise, and I will describe each of them and then give examples of things that I do to help me to live by them. Please feel free to build on these ideas. I also invite you to find your own different methods.

Step One is to start every meeting with another person (or indeed every encounter with our garden or with nature) by being as fully present as possible, and attending to what the other has to communicate to us, both verbally and non-verbally. I try to enter every meeting with an open heart, open mind, and open will, open to what emerges. This involves pausing before I enter a new meeting, noticing my emotions and fears, my thoughts and assumptions, as well as my preconceptions – and letting them go, so that I am ready to be present to what might happen and what might surprise me.

---

8   M. E. Porter and M. R. Kramer (2011) 'Shared value: how to re-invent capitalism and unleash a wave of innovation and growth', *Harvard Business Review*, January: February 2011, Vol. 89, Issue 1/2: 62–77.

9   P. Hawkins (ed.) (2014) *Leadership Team Coaching in Practice*, London: Kogan Page.

Step Two is to witness our responses, thoughts, and feelings while attending to the other, and to share these fully with them. For many years I thought I listened well to other people: after all, I was a trained psychotherapist, counsellor, and coach! Then I discovered that I was only listening with my ears and registering what I heard with my neo-cortex brain. I realised that I had to learn to listen with all of my being, my body as well as my head, my intuition as well as my analytical brain. I slowly realised that for those with whom I was meeting my sharing of what my body and intuition heard was more valuable than what I had understood with the intellectual part of my brain.

Step Three is to listen to the spaces between us and allow the space for grace and for something new to emerge from that space. I recently met with a Chief Executive of a large global company. I was busy trying to understand his many business challenges. He was busy trying to understand my suggestions that might help him. Suddenly I stopped and said: 'We are both busy trying very hard to control these challenges. I wonder what we both need to listen to from the wider system that would help us to move forward together?'

Last year I was honoured to be asked by a lovely couple to take their wedding service. They asked me to attend a joint retreat where we could plan the ceremony together. At the beginning of their retreat I gave them two questions to explore: 'Who and what does your relationship serve?' and 'What is the truth that your relationship needs to speak at your wedding?' By the time we came to co-design the wedding, their work on these two questions made the planning easy and the event itself a joy.

The challenge is to use these practices, not just in protected spaces such as coaching or supervision, or a specially constructed development group, but to find ways of practising reflection in the midst of pressurised and busy action.

Step Four is to bring in to the conversations and meetings the voices of those who are absent or silent. In company board rooms, I will sometimes bring in three empty chairs, one to represent the customers of the organisation, one the employees, and one the investors, so that Board members not only listen to each other dialogically, but also listen to the important stakeholders who are not present. More recently I have also experimented with bringing in a chair for the voice of our 'collective grandchildren', for they will reap the consequences of the decisions that we make today. When conducting weddings or funerals or child blessings, I employ a similar practice: creating space not only for those present, but for absent friends and family, the wider human family, and the more-than-human world.

Conclusion

We need to build into our lives and our work constant reminders to be in the service of the wider systems that constitute the ecology that contains and supports us. The question that we all need to ask, as individuals, congregations, teams, organisations, and as a species is: *'What can we uniquely do that the world of tomorrow needs?'* We need to ask this not just on the grand scale to help us to find our own evolutionary purpose, but moment by moment in our daily lives. We need to constantly ask: 'What is needed right now?' and 'What do I need to shift in my own thinking, being, and doing in order to contribute to a better immediate future for the world that I am part of, right at this moment?'

Most of us are among the most privileged people in the world right now, living in what is probably the most privileged generation that has ever lived. I need constantly to give thanks for all that this has given me, but I need also to realise that privilege brings responsibility. I need to discover daily how I take my values to work and through work constantly evolve and widen my values to embrace the needs of our one human family and the 'more-than-human world'.

Questions for discussion and reflection

The activities suggested below can be done individually but are much more valuable if done as part of a supportive peer group. This might be your family, your religious group, or your work colleagues.

1. Write down a list of your values. I suggest between three and ten.

2. Then for each value write down the behaviours that you would be engaging in if you were exemplifying that value, and what you might be doing that would be contrary to that value.

3. Next recognise that these values are aspirations, and that you will constantly fail to live up to them fully. Forgive yourself in advance.

4. Now think about who can support you in learning and living ethically. With whom can you share these values and behavioural examples? Whom can you invite to give you feedback when they see you positively living up to them, as well as when you are acting contrary to them? Remember that we can all be blind and deaf to the gap between our aspirations and what we do, and we all need critical friends and feedback in order to progress.

5. Explore how you can be more closely aligned with the needs of the 'more-than-human world' – the ecological environment in which you live and which daily supports your life and well-being.

   a. Each day say Thank You for what you have been given by grace from nature.

   b. Find moments when you can bow in reverence and awe to Nature, and experience your connection to it with every part of your being.

   c. Ask yourself what it is that the wider ecology needs human beings to listen to, wake up to, learn, and do differently.

   d. In relation to the answers that you discover in 5(c), develop some simple actions that you can take to make a small but significant difference.

   e. Ask 'What can I uniquely do that the world of tomorrow needs?'

Further reading

Bateson, G. (1972) *Steps to an Ecology of Mind*, London: Paladin Press.

Fox, M. (2000) *Original Blessing*, New York: Tarcher Putnam.

Hawkins, P. (1999) 'Postmodernism and religion', in George D. Chryssides (ed.) *Unitarian Perspectives on Contemporary Religious Thought*, London: Lindsey Press.

Hawkins, P. (2006a) 'A radical revision of Unitarianism for the 21st century', *Faith and Freedom* Vol. 29, Part 2, Number 163, pp. 162–5.

Hawkins, P. (2006b) 'Dialogue as a form of spiritual practice', in Matthew Smith (ed.) *Being Together: Unitarians Celebrate Congregational Life*, London: Lindsey Press.

Heffernan, M. (2011) *Wilful Blindness: Why We Ignore the Obvious at our Peril*, London: Simon and Schuster.

Inayat Khan, H. *Collected Works Volume IV: Mental Purification* (www:http://hazrat-inayat-Khan.org/php/views.php?h1=18&h2=3&h3=0)

The author

Professor Peter Hawkins is a businessman, academic, and consultant who works with organisations throughout the world, helping them to align their strategy, culture, and leadership. He is the author of many books on leadership, coaching, and supervision; and he has also published a number of essays and articles on Unitarian and Sufi spirituality. Peter is a member of the Bath Unitarian Fellowship (www.oldmeeting.org.uk), a Hibbert Trustee, and a teacher, celebrant, and retreat guide in the Universalist Sufi Way (www.sufiway.org).

Engaging with democracy: reflections of a county councillor in rural England

Ruth Archer

I grew to love Unitarianism because of its distinct emphasis on freedom, reason, and tolerance, and I have often thought that the preamble of my political party's constitution is for me a neat way of defining my Unitarianism: '(We) exist to build and safeguard a fair, free and open society in which we seek to balance the fundamental values of liberty, equality and community and in which no one shall be enslaved by poverty, ignorance or conformity.'

Unitarian roots

My Unitarian home is the Great Meeting Leicester, which was influential in the movement for local political reform in the nineteenth century and was known as 'the Mayors' Nest' because so many prominent Unitarians were indeed mayors of Leicester. That tradition has been revived in modern times by city councillor Manjula Sood, who had the distinction in 2008 of being the first Asian female Lord Mayor in the UK, and we can also claim as a member of our congregation the first elected mayor of Leicester City (and former Member of Parliament), Sir Peter Soulsby, who is widely recognised in national Unitarian circles. Perhaps a little bit of that glory rubbed off on me, although my 10 years on Rutland County Council were much more prosaic – but perhaps more achievable for that reason.

One of our most popular hymns at Great Meeting (number 192 in *Hymns For Living*) always lifts my spirit and is a great inspiration:

We would be one as now we join in singing
Our hymn of love, to pledge ourselves anew
To that high cause of greater understanding
Of who we are, and what in us is true.

We would be one in building for tomorrow
A greater world than we have known today;
We would be one in searching for that meaning
Which binds our hearts and points us on our way.

We would be one in living for each other,
With love and justice strive to make all free;
As one, we pledge ourselves in greater service,
To show the world a new community.[1]

I am not a Unitarian by birth. I come from a staunch northern Methodist family, but when our children were small we increasingly felt unable to encourage them, as the old hymn says, to 'trust and obey, there is no other way to be happy in Jesus but to trust and obey'. The 1970s advert in the *Guardian* asking us if we were Unitarians without knowing it led us to Coventry Unitarians, and we immediately felt at home listening to Revd. Hilton Birtles and Revd. Penny Johnson. After a couple of years, a job move to Peterborough sent us into a Unitarian wilderness and we relied on the National Unitarian Fellowship for spiritual sustenance. Several years later we stumbled on Great Meeting, Leicester, coinciding with Revd. Dr Arthur Stewart's first week as the minister there. From then I became a fully active Unitarian and I owe much to Arthur's thought-provoking leadership of our Sunday services.

---

1   The words of this hymn, by the late Revd Samuel Anthony Wright, are in the public domain.

Into politics

My political inclination may well not be very typical of a white middle-class woman living in rural middle England. However, I was a member of the village Parish Council for many years, generally active in the village community and politically active very firmly behind the scenes in the local constituency, stuffing envelopes, delivering leaflets, and putting in many hours of canvassing. We live in Rutland, an affluent county with easily overlooked pockets of rural poverty, which in April 1997 had just regained its independence from Leicestershire. As England's smallest county, Rutland made much of not being run on party-political lines; indeed, most councillors were independents, though very reactionary in outlook, and those of us who took our party politics seriously were rather looked down on.

I stood for election as a county councillor in October 1997, not because I had a burning political ambition to campaign either for or against an important local issue, but simply because a by-election had been called in the ward in which we lived, and I was the only activist in the local party who lived there. I saw it as a challenge, and it was with great trepidation that I put my nomination forward.

I was surprised and quite frankly terrified to have come top of the poll. As the smallest county, with an area slightly bigger than the Isle of Wight, and a population then of only 34,600, with full unitary status, all the services of a local authority such as social care, planning, and education were at that time under the control of just 20 councillors. This meant that if a councillor wanted to do the job properly, she or he had to make a big commitment, because there were so few members, including of course some who sat inactively on the sidelines.

Unitarian values underpinning political action

My Unitarianism was the inspiration which provided the energy and impetus to seize the opportunities that presented themselves with that by-election. Of course there was a tendency for the majority of councillors to greet any new proposal with 'Yes, yes, all very desirable, but not here', or even to respond with a flat 'No' to anything progressive, as can be seen by their attitudes to recycling and Fair Trade goods, which are now accepted by most people as a right and proper use of public money. But winning the by-election was a gateway for me towards using the very limited powers that local democracy had given me, as an ordinary member of the council, to give something back to the community. Tiny steps – yes, but here and there ones that can be seen to have made a positive difference.

I should mention that after a few years the Council did become politicised. The opposition in Rutland comprised a 'ragbag' of parties who scrutinised the work of the large majority who ran the council. However, we did find it difficult to work with one small group who were obsessed with uncovering what the rest of the opposition thought was a mythical web of corruption. It was investigated by the Audit Commission and found to be a complete fabrication. My dissenting Unitarian instincts were sorely tried at this point!

Of course the electors often complain that the council is wrong. This may be a knee-jerk reaction which is perhaps part of our national psyche and will probably never change, nor should it. Careful and fair scrutiny of council business is always something to be valued.

One particular but common problem in political public life is the small number of elected women. For a short time at one point in my 10 years on the council I was the only woman member. The expectation is for female councillors to be involved in 'women's issues', the unspoken implication being, of course, that really difficult subjects such as finance and business projects are matters for the men. This patronising tone was very prevalent in Rutland in my early years on the council, but it actually became a life changer for me. The concept of corporate parenting was introduced by the government in the early years of this century. It was a clear reminder to councillors and officers of their responsibilities for children in care. I was appointed as the Children's Champion, and part of this role was to encourage my fellow councillors to consider the needs of the 'looked after children' *as if they were their own children*. No room for 'Yes, yes, all very desirable, but not here'. It is common for council committee papers to be riddled with statistics, not to mention jargon and obscure acronyms, and this can make the issues seem remote. To bring them to life we invited all the councillors to an informal meeting where a couple of teenagers spoke about what it was actually like to be in care. They were good ambassadors for our foster children, and I like to think that the meeting made a real difference to safeguarding the child-protection budget and making sure that fostered children had access to some of the extras that children from conventional homes took for granted.

We had and still have an excellent group of foster carers in Rutland, and I found that visiting every fostered child once a year was a valuable way to assess whether we councillors were fulfilling our obligations to each child. I served on the adoption panel for the county and on the fostering panel, and I am now an independent member of the fostering panel. Being involved with the marvellous work of the foster carers and the social workers has been a real privilege.

Some particular challenges

My baptism of fire soon after election to the council was a sudden influx of Travellers who took over a section of a green lane on the edge of one of the five villages which then comprised my ward. Questions raised by the legal status of Travellers are in some ways similar to the national and international issues of so-called illegal immigrants. Most of the village, including the farmer whose land and farmhouse were close by, wanted the Travellers moved on immediately. It would have been very easy and popular just to join the locals in hounding them out and to lead a campaign which encouraged people to think of the Travellers as benefit scroungers who wanted to live in the county while not paying any council tax. Although I was new to the sharp end of local politics, my Unitarian instincts told me that this would be unfair, that people should be treated with respect as individuals rather than as stereotypes. Fortunately the law agrees, and my role became the very tricky and unpopular one of explaining to the village that social services, health visitors, and the education department had to check on the well-being of any children and possibly pregnant women, and that this was not a quick process, particularly as more Travellers were attracted to the site and the process was delayed as each new set of caravans arrived. Eventually, the Travellers did what Travellers do and moved on, and of course they then became someone else's problem. But for me their arrival and on-going presence had raised very real and practical questions: do I actually mean it when I endorse the Unitarian principles of Freedom, Reason, and Tolerance? How should I deal with the argument that these people don't deserve public services because they don't pay any tax? My strong belief is that we deserve good public services and that we should be prepared to pay for them for the benefit of all, but I also believe that we should not prevent people adopting an alternative lifestyle.

The local Fair Trade Group raised a much less contentious question. They asked if I would help to make Rutland a Fair Trade County. As a fair-trade enthusiast at Great Meeting, I was happy to help. To get Fair Trade status for a town or city, or in our own case a whole county, the local authority had to make a commitment both to procure fair-trade goods where possible for local-authority premises and to encourage shops, hotels, and other local businesses to do the same. I really did not expect any opposition to this proposal, so I was surprised to hear some councillors argue that we should be supporting our own farmers, not 'foreigners'. I did see fit to ask them to tell me which farms in Rutland grew coffee and tea, and fortunately the common sense of the majority prevailed and Rutland did get its Fair Trade status. Not earth-shaking stuff, but worthwhile steps in the right direction – and of course fair-trade food is commonplace today.

I represented the Council on our local Standing Advisory Council on Religious Education (SACRE). There were representatives from most of the mainstream Christian churches, but not from other faiths, so I was pleased as a Unitarian to be able to bring a multifaith perspective to the group. Although we are predominantly a white community, Rutland is less than 20 miles from multicultural Leicester, and it is of course vital that our children understand and appreciate diversity.

Living sustainably is important to me, and presenting the message of climate change was even more of a massive task 15 years ago than it continues to be today. Some of our small group of opposition councillors were keen to promote kerbside recycling, but we were taken aback when it was clear that one councillor seriously thought we were proposing to recycle the kerbstones! I am sorry to say that we encountered years of resistance to the very idea of recycling waste, simply on the ground of cost. Our council tax is very high, because Rutland's population is so small, and cutting costs year on year was the norm well before the credit crunch took its toll on local-government finances. The best we could do was to keep the proposal alive and the climate-change deniers at bay. Finally it was the national government that came to the rescue by tipping the scales in favour of recycling by forcing councils to pay for the amount of waste which went into landfill. Eventually a fortnightly collection of recyclables was introduced and, with our small enthusiastic team of officers responsible for waste management, Rutland folk rose to the challenge and we are now in the top ten for local-authority recycling rates in the country.

My ten years on the council were personally challenging but hugely rewarding, and although the work that I did was no more than to be expected of any councillor, the thread connecting these reflections from my years of council representation is a belief in the good old-fashioned concepts of freedom, reason, and tolerance, served up with a radical edge.

I would like to encourage others to 'engage in democracy'. Although my political role has now reverted to delivering leaflets and canvassing, my time on the council gave me opportunities on a very small scale here in Rutland to try 'to show the world a new community'. It was well worth it, and it certainly enriched my life.

Questions for discussion and reflection

1. Many people question the value of voting, even though the democratic process is our only defence against extremism and revolution, and many suffragettes gave their lives in its cause. Discuss.

2. How do Unitarian values apply to the balance to be struck between low taxation and the provision of good public services for the whole community?

3. Would you have done things differently in the case of the Travellers? Should they have been evicted immediately?

4. One of Unitarianism's great merits is its ability to give a radical edge when confronting contemporary issues. Do you think that being politically engaged in the local community is an effective way to achieve this?

The author

Ruth trained as an orthoptist at Birmingham Children's Hospital and worked in the West Midlands. She studied for an Open University Arts degree in the 1980s. She is married with two children and four grandchildren.

Ruth was for several years a member of the Vestry of Great Meeting, Leicester (www.leicesterunitarians.co.uk), and she is a past president of the East Midlands Unitarians. She is currently a member of a small working group for the district, exploring how to revive some of our vulnerable chapels.

After winning three elections in ten years, she retired as a county councillor in 2007, but was pleased to be asked to continue serving on the fostering panel as an independent member, and also to serve as a member of the Rutland Access Group, which is concerned with disability-access issues in the county.

Including 'the other'

Paul Kenyon

It is possible that I have explained Unitarian values, or at least my pidgin version of them, to more people in more bizarre circumstances than anyone else in recent times. There was a group of Colonel Gaddafi's men patrolling the Sahara Desert, an Indian driver taking me across the plains of Rajasthan, several groups of migrants making their way across sub-Saharan Africa, and – the most difficult audience of all – a bar full of journalists in East Ukraine.

I work as a correspondent for BBC Panorama and have spent the last twenty years travelling and reporting, often on various forms of human misery. It's not that I go around searching for people who might want to listen to my views on faith; it's just that in many of these places, particularly in life-or-death situations, a person's religion often defines them, and so people are understandably intent on discovering mine.

'You're from England, yes? You're Christian, yes?'

'Well,' I say, tentatively, *'not quite'.*

And so begins a question-and-answer session which begins with puzzlement ('So what is your Book?... Do you celebrate Easter?...Was Jesus the son of God?') and often ends with the statement 'That's me! That's what I believe in too. I just didn't know there was a name for it.'

I tell them that in the chapel of my childhood we had sermons which quoted the Koran and allowed us to consider the merits of Buddhism, Hinduism, and even atheism. 'I was allowed to choose what was right for me', I say. 'It wasn't about learning a book and believing every word. It took a bit more effort than that, a bit more thought.'

I am fortunate, I have realised in recent years, that I did not have to search for my faith: it came to me. I was born into a family of Unitarians and attended Bury Unitarian Church from an early age. I have Catholic friends who are mesmerised by the idea that I was not *forced* to believe in anything at all, that I could choose. It's the freedom that appeals to them, the freedom to question and criticise and challenge. They, like others, find the idea liberating.

But there is one set of people that I have spent time with whose predicament makes me more aware of my faith than most. These are people who have lost everything and belong nowhere, people who are persecuted and abused until the light within them has almost gone. I am talking about migrants escaping from conflict or, more often, fleeing chronically poor and chaotic lives which offer little hope of change. For the BBC, I spent a year following some of them along the world's most dangerous migration route, out of sub-Saharan Africa, across thousands of miles of desert, and then across the Mediterranean Sea towards Europe. There are no statistics for how many die on that route, but the estimate from aid agencies is around one in four.

* * * *

When we came over the top of the dune, we saw our first body. It was lying behind a low grey rock, with a wrap of dried cloth curled around its head. I crouched down beside it and saw that it was the body of a young man, probably in his twenties; it was hard to say – the sun had fused the wrap on to his face. He lay on his back, his feet in the narrow shadow of the rock, the rest of his body in the full blaze of the Saharan sun. His hands were thrown to either side. In one of them he held an empty plastic water bottle.

We had set off a few days earlier, from a town called Effiakuma on Ghana's Cape Coast. I had sat there in the town's white clay mosque, listening to the Imam tell the young men: 'Those who take this route, we call them heroes.' The fittest, he said, the cream of the community, should try to get to Europe, so they could send money home to support the rest of the village. 'It's like a war', he said. 'We are fighting poverty and illiteracy and poor health.'

So, days later when I crouched beside that dead body, I had some idea of how the young man had ended up on a Libyan sand dune, thousands of miles from home, and another thousand or so from where he wanted to be. Standing beside me was a Libyan border patrol guard, cradling an old hunting rifle, and signalling that it was time to go.

'*You want to say a prayer for him?*' I asked.

The guard screwed up his face, shook his head, and began to climb back up the dune. '*He's not one of us*', he shouted back.

'*What do you mean? Not Libyan?*'

'*No, not Muslim.*'

'*How do you know?*' I shouted back. '*Most of these guys are Muslim, and anyway why would it matter?*'

'*If he's not Muslim, I wouldn't pray for him*', he said, and then disappeared over the crest of the dune.

To the border guard, this man was an outsider, not just ethnically and culturally, but spiritually too. The guard's job was to keep this man out of Libya, and either send him back or shoot him. But in death too the guard had excluded the migrant. His religion, or at least his interpretation of it, did not allow him to tolerate anyone else's, so he could show no compassion. He was a border guard both for the living and for the dead. I stood beside the body and said something quietly about hoping his suffering had come to an end, and that his family would be able to find strength. It was somewhere between prayer and reflection. I suspect that my cameraman thought the sun had got to me.

The guard's intolerance of outsiders was based on a familiar theme: that of protecting what belongs to us, to our families, to our communities. Migrants *take* jobs, they *take* living space, they *take* medical care, they *take* our social-security benefits, they *take* the purity from our religious doctrine. And the more migrants there are, the more taking there is. And the more taking there is, the less remains for the rest of us. That, as far as I can see, seems to be the nub of it.

That evening, around a campfire in the desert, I explained that my experience taught me differently: that migrants try to find work, to contribute to society, that they have made sacrifices on the journey which tell us much about what they have left behind, and that, in the end, the added diversity can only enrich our lives. I am not sure that this was a result of my Unitarian faith. It is impossible to disentangle that from the liberal values that my parents encouraged more generally. But the guard who had refused to pray was there, and I know that my words set them all thinking.

On that same route, I came across an event so remarkable that I wrote a book about it. A group of migrants who had survived the desert crossing attempted what tens of thousands of others do each year: they squeezed themselves into a makeshift boat and tried to cross the Mediterranean Sea for Europe. When they were fifty miles from land, their boat began to sink. None of them could swim. They managed to steer their vessel towards a tuna fishing net, before it finally went down. Then, all 26 of them scrambled on to the buoys of the net and clung on for the next three days and nights.

At the end of the first night they ran out of water. Some started drinking from the sea, others fell in and were pulled out by their hysterical friends. Many thought that the tuna in the net were man-eating fish. Some were only semi-conscious. A Muslim survivor told me that they took it in turns to pray to their own gods. 'If the Christians were right,' he said, 'then we would all be saved too, because we were all together on the same net.' In the end they sang together, Christians, Muslims, and those who just believed in magic: 'Please god save us', again and again.

They were eventually picked up by the Italian navy. When I met them, they were desperate and hungry and homeless. As we were filming with them, we gave them food, and sometimes money. Over the weeks and months that followed, they would contact me, sometimes weeping, and ask for more. To me, it seemed only fair that, as they had given us their stories (the only thing they had), I should try to help. But, of course, the giving just encouraged them to ask for more. It went on. Then one of them said if that I didn't send him money he would kill the next person he saw.

My initial response, of tolerance and generosity, turned sour. I refused to speak with any of them again. Friends would say to me, 'We told you, they're all the same, all on the take!', and although I have never accepted that, I have to admit that for a while it did affect my perception of migrants on that route. It was a struggle to remind myself that, in this group, the slyness, the nastiness, and the brutality were a product of what they had been through, because of their genuine desperation. Even as I write this, I am thinking that a truly selfless person would have understood and accepted that, and would have continued to help. But that is where I drew the line.

Some time later, the British tabloids turned their firepower on the new migration menace: East Europeans. In the Berkshire town of Slough, I went searching for Romanians and Bulgarians 'flocking' to the area as EU work restrictions were lifted. The manager of a local hardware shop pointed to a double-page spread in his red-top newspaper.

'This is where they're all coming', he said. *'Look, it says Slough is a hotspot!'* And then: *'I'm telling you there's going to be trouble in these streets.'*

'Who is it, in particular, you don't like?' I asked.

He paused for a moment. *'It's just the Romanians, to be honest with you.'*

'Why the Romanians?' I asked.

He struggled for a while and then said, *'They're just not the same as us.'*

'And what about you?' I asked. *'Your family...'.* It felt uncomfortable to point out the obvious. *'Where are you from, Pakistan?'*

'Yes', he nodded, without acknowledging any irony. *'My father came here from Pakistan, but when our people came here, they came to work hard, they adapted, they made money, and now we are as good as anyone else.'*

Here he was, an outsider who had become an insider, and was now adopting insider hostility against the new outsiders. Again, for him, it was about protecting his own from those who he believed had come to *take* what was not theirs. He had achieved status, ownership, acceptance, no doubt at some significant cost, but he could not find it within himself to help others who were now following the same path.

I tried to explain, gently, that one day the Romanian migrants might feel the same way as him, when the next 'wave of migrants' hits our shores. I tried to suggest that perhaps it was not really the Romanians he was concerned about, but just any outsiders trying to better themselves; that their nationality was irrelevant.

But to him, and to others, I have often found the notion of 'including the other' a difficult one to sell. People are deeply fearful of 'the other' taking what is theirs, and sometimes for understandable reasons if they are from conflict zones, or places where the roar of poverty deafens out reason, or even in the UK, where austerity and unemployment might have left some people looking for a group of outsiders to blame.

The more recent migration crisis, with record numbers of refugees arriving in Europe from Syria, Afghanistan, and Eritrea, has given a new dimension to negative notions of 'the other'. In the spring of 2015, when it was clear that this was a movement of people like no other since World War II, there was the familiar response: suspicion, hostility, a call to reject the migrants and protect our country, our culture, our economy. But then a photograph appeared which quickly changed the national mood. It showed the lifeless body of a baby washed up on a Turkish beach – a human being so blameless, so vulnerable, and also so familiar. He looked like any other baby, in a pair of tiny shoes with a little red t-shirt, face down on the beach as though he were sleeping. And he had a name. Aylan. Now millions could identify with the father and his loss. Aylan looked like their child, any child. He had moved the perception of migrants from 'the other' to 'one of us'.

Questions for discussion and reflection

1. *Is fear of immigration something deeper than a concern about outsiders taking what is ours?* It is interesting that the UK government is currently trying to encourage more Chinese and Russian oligarchs to come to Britain, while tightening the rules against other nationalities. Britain is accepting far fewer migrants in the current crisis than its European neighbours, even since the photograph of Aylan emerged. The Prime Minister is trying to appear tough on migration because he senses that there is still a mood of suspicion and he knows that many blame migrants for failings in the NHS, housing, and other services. But why was Germany prepared to accept 800,000 in one year, when Britain offered to take just 20,000 over five years? Do German political leaders not care about the pressure on services in Germany? Of course they do, but they also know that migrants are, in the long run, a net benefit to the country's economy.

2. In the end, it comes down to wealth. We are content for people to settle in Britain if they invest, because we think that means that they are not 'taking'. But *is wealth really a fair measure of someone's suitability to remain in the UK?*

3. *How should we deal with giving?* I tried to help a group of migrants, and I came under increasing pressure. I tried to get charities and the UNHCR to help, but they were already overwhelmed. I even tried to help some of the group to get jobs. Was it kinder, in the long run, to pull back, and let them find their own way?

Further reading, and watching

Paul Kenyon (2009) *I am Justice: A Journey Out of Africa*, published by Preface, and available on Amazon.

Europe or Die Trying: a Panorama TV programme on the migration journey described in this chapter. This programme, as well as *Destination Europe, Destination UK*, and *Children of the Great Migration*, can be seen on Youtube.

The author

Paul Kenyon is a BAFTA-winning journalist and author who has reported from around the world for the BBC. He is also a Unitarian, and son of the former President of the General Assembly, Neville Kenyon. Paul is a veteran of investigative journalism. He has exposed child labour in Cambodia and Côte d'Ivoire, and corrupt pharmaceutical companies in India. He confronted one of Gaddafi's sons over war crimes in Libya. Paul was also one of the first journalists to follow the most dangerous migration route in the world, from Africa across the Mediterranean Sea. He made several films about those risking their lives to make the journey: a body of work that has received awards from the Royal Television Society. He also wrote a book about the experience: *I Am Justice: A Journey Out of Africa*. Paul says that throughout his career he has tried to give a voice to the vulnerable, poor, and defenceless.

Embodying equality
Ann Peart

A Unitarian upbringing

Living in a way that supports and encourages those less privileged than me is something to which I aspire, but which I do not always achieve. As a child brought up in a nominally Unitarian family, and as a teenager who became a chapel attender and keen reader of Unitarian pamphlets, my values have always been Unitarian in ethos. A sense of fair play developed into a respect for justice and a sense of 'the worth and dignity of all people', coupled with a typically British urge to side with the under-dog.

One of my early memories is of being taken to a Manchester railway station to meet an aunt with her Pakistani husband when they came to live in England. It was some years before I learned that my uncle had been a political prisoner in Pakistan because of his communist activities; and not until his funeral, when Tariq Ali praised Afzal as his hero and wrote the *Guardian* obituary, did I learn what a significant role my uncle had played. But from an early age I knew that it was wrong to discriminate against people because of their skin colour.

The first time I was personally aware of gender injustice was in my first paid work, a holiday job at the small engineering works run by my family. I was an office junior earning two shillings an hour, while my younger brother was on the factory floor, an all-male preserve, earning six pence per hour more than me.

Although my parents insisted on my having an education of equal quality to my brother's, and we both went to university, the different social roles that were ascribed to us became increasingly obvious, and patterns set in the early 1960s informed my married life until divorce in the late 1970s. Then second-wave feminism, in particular women's consciousness-raising groups, helped me to realise just how unfair society was to women in general. Although I had a better degree and more qualifications than my ex-husband, my earning power was considerably less, and it was assumed that I would look after the children from the marriage, as well as earn my living.

The influence of Golders Green Unitarians

The personal did indeed become political and religious, as I realised how the male-dominated language used in churches reinforced the subordination of women. Golders Green Unitarians, my local congregation, led by the Revd. Keith Gilley, were in the forefront of equality work, particularly in relation to women and to sexuality, and I joined in this with enthusiasm. (Some of this story is told in my contributions to earlier Lindsey Press publications, edited by George Chryssides.) The more I became involved in equality projects, at personal, local, and national levels, the deeper my awareness of inequality became. One such national project was the Unitarian Working Party on Feminist Theology, consisting of six people, including myself, working together for several years to produce a report which was published in 1984. This was an early attempt to look at the way in which traditional religious words and practices have affected the status of women, and it is still the only such work promoted by our General Assembly. Women in the Golders Green congregation and in the wider London movement began to explore women's issues within Unitarianism, and in 1981 we launched a national Unitarian Women's Group which still continues this work.

Locally, the Golders Green congregation had helped to establish one of the earliest branches of Amnesty International. My active role in this group certainly put my uncle's imprisonment into the wider perspective of international human-rights abuses. That same congregation, again led by Keith Gilley, and joined by Dudley Cave, a member of the congregation who was prominent in the gay community, took a lead in promoting equality for gay men and lesbians. As a married woman in the 1970s I had enjoyed attending Integroup, a pioneering group consisting of both homosexual and heterosexual people (no questions asked), who met monthly at the Golders Green Church and explored a variety of topics concerning sexuality and gender, with some very impressive speakers. The group closed in the 1980s, but by then it had done much to ensure that gay men and lesbians were welcome in the congregation. So when, as the newish minister at that congregation, I came out as lesbian in the early 1990s, there was very little reaction, except to be happy that I had found a loving partner.

Sexuality

Nationally the Unitarians set up a working party to work on a programme to help congregations to address questions of equality and sexuality. The Sexual Orientation Equality Group, of which I was a member, produced a resource pack, entitled *Celebrating Diversity*, in 2003. Members of the group presented workshops in congregations up and down the country. The practice was to send two people, one gay and one straight, to lead the events. One of the other women members and I used to enjoy the puzzled reactions when it was the lesbian who mentioned having children; those who did not know us could not work out which was the heterosexual one and which the lesbian – a useful lesson in itself.

A similar situation occurred much later, when a group was taking part in the Manchester Gay Pride parade as *Unitarians Valuing Diversity*. Most of the ministers were wearing clerical collars to indicate that our ministry as well as our general membership is open to all, and although most of the group were gay, lesbian, or bisexual, we were supported by several heterosexual friends. As usual, the fundamentalist anti-gay Christians were on the pavement with their banners and slogans invoking God's wrath on all deviants. Unfortunately one of them got over the barrier and started haranguing the Unitarians, concentrating on one particular minister. But the protestor did not realise that the person selected for his verbal attack, prophesying hell and damnation, was not gay, but happily married to someone of the opposite sex! As he was a trade unionist and well able to deal with hecklers without any help, the rest of us looked on with amusement.

Ministry and worship

Gender
Equality has been a conscious element in my ministry over the years, including the conduct of worship. The GA feminist theology group, in conjunction with the then Worship Sub-committee, led workshops to promote the use of inclusive language, which coincided with the publication in 1985 of *Hymns for Living*, the first denominational hymn book in the UK to apply inclusive language to subjects both human and divine. I take care to ensure that the words that I use do not appear to value or deify one sex only. Although in *Growing Together* Revd. Dr. Arthur Long made a compelling case for inclusive language as early as 1984, I find that even today too many people leading worship do not take this matter seriously, referring to God as he, or as Lord, without realising the subtle message of female unworthiness and exclusion that this conveys. If I am conducting worship for a congregation that customarily says the Lord's Prayer together, I take along a modern gender-inclusive version to use instead. One that I often use (with some amendments) is taken from *Intimations of Grandeur* by the Unitarian Universalist Jacob Trapp[1] – although I confess that if the prayer is sung rather than spoken, I do not try to change it, to avoid disrupting the music and the flow of the service. So I lack consistency in putting my principles into practice. However, I do try to ensure that the sources for my service are not entirely male dominated; but appropriateness for the occasion is the main criterion, and it is still sometimes difficult to find suitable readings and prayers written by women.

Participation
Often I have been able to develop a more participatory style, with people in the congregation contributing something of themselves to the service. In my year as President of the Unitarian General Assembly I conducted many services throughout Britain and found that two particular practices

---

1   Jacob Trapp (1968) *Intimations of Grandeur; Meditations*, London: Lindsey Press.

worked well. For district occasions I evolved a service in which someone from each congregation spoke briefly about something precious in their tradition and offered one hope for the future, often symbolising their contribution by placing a stone or lighting a candle. This enabled people from the different congregations to hear each other, learn about themselves, and make a small step towards creating a more inclusive community, as the small congregations were given as much voice and attention as the larger ones. One drawback of such participation is that some voices are not always audible to the entire congregation, and there is a danger of excluding anyone with less than perfect hearing, so this has to be managed carefully, by inviting contributors to face the congregation, and using a roving microphone if available. The same opportunities and difficulties apply to the sharing of joys and concerns in the lighting of candles, a custom gradually spreading among our congregations.

The address
A third way in which I try to promote equality in preparing worship is in the quotations and illustrations used during the address. It is so easy to employ examples of 'normal' families where the assumption of two parents (mother and father) and probably two children is implicit, if not directly stated. Yet this is a minority situation in Britain. For much of my children's childhood they were living in a single-parent home, seeing their father only occasionally. This made me very aware when composing services that it is not necessarily appropriate to assume a two-parent household. More people live alone, and/or have less than easy situations with their relatives, be they children, parents, grandparents, siblings or cousins. I try to mirror this in the illustrations and stories that form part of the address.

College Principal

Some of my ministry was spent working as the Principal of Unitarian College, Manchester, where Unitarian ministers and lay pastors are prepared for ministry. It took me some time to develop a more feminist, egalitarian style of management. When I came into the post, the college's educational side was run on what my predecessor had called 'gentlemen's agreement' lines, with no clear written procedures, and a role for the Principal resembling the patriarchal head of a family. I introduced written learning agreements, and grievance and disciplinary procedures, so that we all knew where we stood, and the Principal's decisions were not arbitrary. This may not seem like a step towards equality, but I think that, coupled with greater opportunities for participation, giving students as much freedom as possible to choose their own courses within the limits of feasibility and General Assembly requirements, it gave students more power over their training. I also re-formed an advisory academic subcommittee, so that I was not making decisions about students' courses on my own, but in consultation with the other Unitarian tutors and the committee chair. I also tried to be open to the inclusion of occasional students, and people interested in training for lay leadership rather than full-time professional ministry.

Each week the students came from various parts of the country to spend one or two days in college. I developed the practice of starting with an in-gathering, serving tea, coffee, and cake to create an atmosphere of welcome and hospitality, as well as giving everyone an opportunity to share something of how they were feeling. In planning the details of the curriculum, I tried to ensure that the students became aware of issues of gender and sexuality. For example, I made great efforts to include women's writings in the courses on Unitarian history and thought, and when students prepared work for seminars on these areas they were asked to include sources written by women. In the rites-of-passage course we included material on same-sex blessings, as well as other more unusual transitions. (This was before same-sex couples could choose legal marriage or civil partnership.) We usually ended the course by students conducting a different sort of transition ritual, and one of the most moving was a ceremony designed to be conducted in the home for someone undergoing gender re-assignment.

Historian

A distinctive area of my ministry is researching and writing on Unitarian topics, mainly on Unitarian women, but also on issues of sexuality and equality. It seemed to me that the continuing male bias in Unitarian writing needed to be addressed, and one way of doing this was to enable Unitarian women to have access to what Letty Russell has described as a 'useable past'. She wrote: 'Research into the hidden past of oppressed people frees them to gain a sense of history on which to build their future'.[2] So my historical writings are a deliberate attempt to work for gender justice within the Unitarian movement. This has meant not only discovering stories of the lives of Unitarian women and placing them alongside those of men, but uncovering some of the ways in which women were ignored or silenced, and investigating how women influenced the movement in ways still not appreciated by most men. It took me ten years to finish my PhD thesis, but the discipline has been helpful in many ways, not least in opening my eyes to methodologies which expose and counter injustice and inequality. My thesis included case studies of three Unitarian women, Anna Barbauld (1743–1825), an influential poet and writer on education, religion, and civil rights; Helen Martineau (née Bourn, later Tagart, 1795–1871), a typical Unitarian middle-class woman of the time, who is known only through her personal letters; and Frances Power Cobbe (1822–1904), an Irish convert to Unitarianism who was a prominent writer, journalist, and campaigner for women's and animals' rights. Later writings include articles on other Unitarian women, and both lay women and women ministers in the Unitarian movement.

Conclusion

So far this chapter has referred only to specific initiatives; but a world of increasing inequality demands also a certain quality of being. It is

2 Letty M. Russell (1974) *Human Liberation in a Feminist Perspective – A Theology*, Philadelphia, USA: Westminster Press.

in day-to-day living that I try to witness to equality. Climate change will affect the poor people in the world far more than the rich, so reducing my carbon footprint and trying to live more simply is part of my spiritual practice, as is buying fairly traded and organic goods where practicable. The British government's austerity policy is driving more children and women into poverty, so highlighting and opposing this is becoming a priority. Its anti-terrorist campaign against 'radicalisation' is in danger of demonising all Muslims, so interfaith connections and the local 'Hope Not Hate' campaign also have my support, often in minor ways such as simply exchanging a friendly word or smile.

Questions for discussion and reflection

1. What signs of increasing inequality have you noticed in your local area and in the world at large?

2. How do you as an individual work for greater equality? What more could you do?

3. How does your congregation work for greater equality? What more could it do?

4. What organisations are active locally in promoting equality?

Further reading

Croft, Joy (ed.) 1984 *Growing Together: The Report of the Unitarian Working Party on Feminist Theology*, London: General Assembly of Unitarian and Free Christian Churches (available on the GA website).

Long, Arthur (1984) 'Sexist Language' in Croft, Joy (ed.) op.cit.

Peart, Ann (1999) 'Forgotten Prophets: Unitarian Women and Religion' in George Chryssides (ed.) *Unitarian Perspectives on Contemporary Religious Thought*, London: Lindsey Press, pp. 61–76.

Peart, Ann (2003) 'Of Warmth and Love and Passion: Unitarians and (Homo) sexuality' in George D. Chryssides (ed.) *Unitarian Perspectives on Contemporary Social Issues*, London: Lindsey Press, pp. 60–76.

Peart, Ann (2006) 'Forgotten Prophets; The Lives of Unitarian Women 1760–1904', PhD Thesis, University of Newcastle. Accessible online at https://theses.ncl.ac.uk/dspace/bitstream/10443/245/1/peart05.pdf

Sexual Orientation Equality Group (2003) *Celebrating Diversity: A Resource Pack for Unitarian and Free Christian Leaders on Sexual Orientation and Other Equality Issues,* London: General Assembly of Unitarian and Free Christian Churches.

The author

Ann Peart was born into a northern, nominally Unitarian family, and began attending chapel from the age of 12. Her first significant role was as the May Queen of her local congregation, when she developed a taste for ministry, and she has been active in the Unitarian movement ever since. A degree in Geography from New Hall Cambridge was followed by years of school teaching, marriage, and motherhood, until divorce gave her the opportunity to train for the ministry. Ministries in London, including a period as the Information Officer at Unitarian headquarters, were followed by several years in the post of Principal of Unitarian College, Manchester, from which she retired in 2009.

Ann has held many voluntary positions in the Unitarian movement, including presidencies of the Women's League, Historical Society, Ministerial Fellowship, Manchester District, and the (British) General Assembly of Unitarian and Free Christian Churches.

The subject of her PhD was Unitarian women, and she has researched widely on this subject. She co-founded the feminist Unitarian Women's Group, and has been active in LGBT and feminist causes. She is currently a member of Cross Street Chapel, Manchester.

Championing the environment and greening the spirit
Alex Brianson

Introduction: stop, look, and listen

The truly lovely thing about epiphanies is that they come unbidden. I have always devoured books for pleasure, provocation, and instruction, so I guess the odds were always that I would stumble across some form of enlightenment in black and white. But I did not expect it that afternoon in my partly converted loft-space office, reading a book in a discipline other than my own. But there it was: the voice of Arne Næss, the Norwegian philosopher, calling to me from beyond the grave. Something amazing happened to my mind, my heart, and my soul that day; it was my own private Damascene conversion, and I will always be grateful for it.

I had long sought a way to acknowledge and make sense of my spirituality but had failed to find it in many years of searching various traditions, although I did unearth something helpful in almost all those that I tried (the sole exception being a discussion with a very severe, desiccated Buddhist nun). In my late thirties, this quest was becoming more important to me; life had given me a few scars, as it tends to do, and I wanted to find a greater sense of meaning and purpose. I had also begun a conscious re-thinking of my understanding of the world around me, and in particular of the non-human species in it. Over the previous few years I had realised the extent to which consciousness and agency exist in species other than our own. I had learned this from an unexpected teacher: a black Labrador-cross called Bob, who shared my life for thirteen years. I learned to understand how he was communicating, and to see purposive thought in much of what he did. I loved him deeply and fiercely.

So, back to the loft on *that* afternoon. I have always been interested in environmental politics, and I worked for a short while as a policy maker in that area before beginning an academic career in political science. I had started a project which attempted to bridge the gaps between my two areas of research, European Union politics and the environment, and I was reading around in environmental philosophy. And there it was: Næss's concept of Deep Ecology, which argued that all living beings have inherent value, that humans must be motivated by love for the natural world as well as love for our own species, and that radical political, social, and economic change is necessary if our planet is to continue to support not just our planet-mates across the species barrier but also our human civilisation. Næss also advocated that all who accept the tenets of Deep Ecology must act in the world for progressive ecological change. I was smitten, particularly with the ideas of inherent value in all living beings, and the need for political engagement based upon spiritual conviction. Suddenly, for me everything was joined up: politics, spirituality, and philosophy in a combination that made sense. This realisation was a caesura of epic proportions: my life really can be divided into 'before' and 'after' periods, with the Afternoon of Arne as the fulcrum.

Since that day, I have spent my time trying to develop a new perspective on my life, and on life in general. If matter and spirit, not to mention humanity and the rest of nature, are locked together, then what we need to develop is an understanding of ourselves, our society, and the global ecosystem that can reflect this fundamental, or *integral*, unity. The American scholar Karen Litfin puts this very accessibly: an integral perspective is one which 'understand(s)...the universe as a revelation or manifestation of consciousness, Spirit or intelligence...(because) mind and matter are two dimensions of a single reality that expresses itself in the self-organizing process of the universe' (Litfin 2003: 33). In what follows, I discuss how I have attempted to respond to this challenge, which coincided with my becoming a Unitarian. But before then, I discuss how environmentalism shapes my daily life.

Everyday environmentalism

I would love to say that I live a completely 'green' life; but if I did, I would be a liar. This is partly because, as the old truism has it, nobody's perfect. But it is also a consequence of the way in which our society and economy are organised. A good example is commuting: the only viable way to get from where I live to where I work is by car, and although in all my previous jobs I have been able to live close enough to walk, cycle, or take the bus, in my current job none of those is a suitable option, and moving closer has not proved possible. This has caused me great grief: I hate adding to the levels of CO_2 emissions, and to air-pollution levels, just to get to work. Thankfully this particular problem is coming to an end soon, and I have vowed never to commute again, but the damage that I have caused to the environment in the last four years cannot be undone. Until we have a more sustainable transport policy, linked to a re-localising of economic life, there is a limit to what many of us can do in this regard. This is why I believe it is vital that we all do what we can, right now; if we wait until we can do everything, it will be far too late.

I have been a vegetarian since I was 15, and although I chose this way to feed myself for animal-welfare reasons, I continue it for climate-change reasons too. Because of the way meat is produced through industrial farming, and the quantity of 'livestock' that is involved, it is a huge contributor to climate-changing gas emissions. Giving up meat is one of the easy things that almost anyone in the first world can do to become more impact-neutral in environmental terms. I make other choices about what I buy, and how I live, for similar reasons. For instance, my electricity is bought from Ecotricity, a renewable-energy company; I buy second-hand whenever I can for things like furniture and books; I support small, local businesses rather than multinational corporations whenever possible, and buy as many organic and/or fair-trade variants of the things I need as I can afford. I have bought ecologically sound laundry, cleaning, and washing-up products for years, most of the time, and nowadays eco-friendly shampoo and soap are much more widely available and affordable, so I get those too. There is a supermarket that I can walk to, so most of the time I use it instead of driving to an alternative, even though it means that I go more often.

The harder, more committed side of my environmentalism goes deeper than reducing consumption and being a 'greener' shopper. I have educated myself in green political theory and philosophy, to the point at which I can and do teach postgraduate students in these areas. Over the years I have been very active in the Green Party and have supported many NGOs in the environmental protection field. This has required a long-term commitment to spend time and money trying to effect political, social, and economic change. At times, the slowness of this work has driven me to despair, and to temporary burn-out. But after a rest and a chance to recuperate, I have bounced back, and have also been able to use these experiences to deepen my spiritual understanding.

How does my environmentalism shape my Unitarianism?

Before joining a Unitarian church, I knew very little about the denomination. I had Unitarian friends who did not talk about their beliefs very much, and another who only 'came out' to me as a Unitarian after I had told him about my own discovery of the movement. For me, Unitarianism has been a consciously chosen religion, discovered well into adulthood after many of my moral or ethical convictions were already well formed. I needed a spiritual home which could help me to deepen my exploration of my inner world and psyche, but I also needed this sanctuary to be dedicated to social and political progress, matching inner exploration with contributions to the achievement of a better and more just society. These issues may not motivate everyone, and, as hinted above, I fully accept that often the best – and maybe the sole – thing we can do in the face of social resistance to a paradigm shift is to change *ourselves*. For me, however, they are very important matters, and they are at the heart of environmentalism. As a result I was delighted to discover that Unitarians are akin to Quakers in having a proud tradition of progressive social and political campaigning.

Green philosophy, as expounded by Næss and others, is devoted to thinking for oneself. It offers understandings of how the world is, and what it is, and what we are, but like any philosophy it asks us to ponder and reflect upon its nostrums and decide for ourselves if they are helpful or ring true. This is a stance that I have always adopted in my professional life as an academic, but it also reflects how I was brought up. For me, this emphasis on thinking critically for oneself is precious. I am very willing to be guided by anyone who has lessons to teach me, and I have often been deeply grateful for their wisdom, as I certainly do not have good answers to all life's questions myself. However, I also refuse automatically to accept belief systems wholesale; if I find a problem with a philosophical or political argument, I can't overlook it, and I will seek a means to resolve the difficulty. If I fail, then I reject the argument, albeit with the proviso that I might change my mind later if that seems appropriate. I needed a religion that not only allowed this approach but fostered it, and Unitarianism has been wonderful in this regard. I have taken part in several Unitarian discussion groups that have helped the participants to think through what they believe and why, without seeking to impose any particular credo. I have loved this, and am very aware that my spiritual evolution could easily have stopped without it.

A further way in which my environmentalism has shaped my Unitarianism is in the fondness it has given me for Universalism, which for me is the belief that the Divine can be understood in many ways, and thus that all religions are likely to have something to contribute to our quest for an ethical, spiritually rich way of life. I have for many years been attracted to elements of Buddhist philosophy, but also to many aspects of Wiccan and neo-pagan religion. When I think of the Divine in personal terms, I think of Her as a Goddess more often than not. For me, the act of creation – birthing the Universe – sits more logically with the idea of a female deity than a male one, and this is something that Unitarianism can accept, even if not all Unitarians would subscribe to it. This Universalism has also enabled me to re-engage with Christian thought. I still struggle with much of this, but my mind is much more open towards it than it was: I have been spurred on to further reading by the realisation that if Universalism is right and all religions have some potential to help us spiritually, then that must be as true for the Christianity that I had long rejected as for religions that I knew less well. In particular, the Creation Spirituality movement led by Matthew Fox, which places Christianity in an environmentalist context, has proved inspirational to me.

Perhaps the final way in which environmentalism has shaped my Unitarian practice and belief is in its love for the created world. Although Green philosophy has much to say about responsibility, and giving proper weight to the interests of other species, not just other humans, it also has much to say about pleasure and joy. I think it is impossible to love the world and not revel in its beauty, or relish the sensual pleasures of being alive.

How does my Unitarianism shape my environmentalism?

And what about the opposite direction of travel: does my Unitarianism shape my environmentalism? In short, the answer is 'yes', in three key ways. First, having a religious anchor for my life has helped me to maintain conviction and hope in the face of ecological disaster such as human-made climate change, over-population, and species extinction. Without my Unitarianism, I am not sure that I would still be as committed as I am to Green politics; all the scientific evidence touches the head, but it is our human senses of aesthetics, morality, awe, and wonder that reach the *heart*.

In addition, Unitarianism, and belonging to a Unitarian community, has helped me to be open about my passion for the spiritual aspects of political ecology; it gives me a sense of security that I can act in a world, especially a professional world, which seems wedded to the idea that there is no need for spirituality. It is much easier to say things that challenge the dominant materialist perspective when you are sure there is always going to be a group of people who won't assume that such a challenge automatically defines you as insane.

My Unitarianism also helps me to keep going when I know I have fallen short or failed to live up to my principles. Living in a 'green' way is difficult in contemporary society; there is a great deal that we can all do, but truly sustainable lives are probably beyond us without radical collective social change. Unitarianism helps me to remember that the struggle is important even when results seem far off, and it also helps me to remember to treat my human failings more kindly than I did in my youth.

Questions for reflection and discussion

1. Do you believe that only humans have consciousness? If so, why? If not, how do you reflect this belief in your Unitarian practice and everyday life?

2. 'Forfeit your sense of awe, let your conceit diminish your ability to revere, and the universe becomes a marketplace for you' (Rabbi Heschel). What do you make of this claim that spirituality is linked to sensuousness and an appreciation of creation/the world in which we live?

3. Which religious or spiritual writers move you most? What do they teach about the relationship between humans and the rest of nature, and the responsibilities of humans to and for the environment?

Further reading

Akuppa (2009) *Saving the Earth: A Buddhist View,* Cambridge: Windhorse Publications. (A very easy-to-read guide to Buddhism and environmentalism, which includes a helpful checklist of important but everyday things we can all do to live more sustainably.)

Fox, M. (1991) *Creation Spirituality: Liberating Gifts for the Peoples of the Earth,* New York: HarperCollins. (The book that I have found most helpful in understanding the Christian tradition from a green perspective.)

Litfin, K. (2003) 'Towards an Integral Perspective on World Politics: Secularism, Sovereignty and the Challenge of Political Ecology', *Millennium: Journal of International Relations* 32:1, 29–56. (A journal article which shaped my own academic work.)

Litfin, K. (2014) *Eco-villages: Lessons for Sustainable Community,* Cambridge: Polity Press. (An intriguing and accessible book, part-memoir and part-manifesto.)

Macy, J. (2007) *World as Lover, World as Self: Courage for Global Justice and Ecological Renewal,* Berkeley, CA: Parallax Press. (A book which helped me to understand Buddhism in a new way, linking it with environmentalism and political activism.)

Næss, A. (1989) *Ecology, Community and Lifestyle: Outline of an Ecosophy,* Cambridge: Cambridge University Press. (A work of academic philosophy, but much more accessible than that makes it sound.)

Taylor, B. (2010) *Dark Green Religion: Nature Spirituality and the Planetary Future,* Berkeley, CA: University of California Press. (A really interesting overview of how ecology and religion can sit together, written intelligibly by a leading expert in the field.)

www.deepecology.org
The website of the Deep Ecology foundation.

www.greenspirit.org.uk
The website of GreenSpirit, a UK-based organisation dedicated to greening our lives and spirituality.

The author

Alex Brianson is a former Professor of Politics. He has been a Unitarian for about seven years and lives near Portsmouth. A member of the Green Party, he is also on the advisory board of Green House, a think-tank devoted to finding effective ways to 'green' the way we live: www.greenhousethinktank. org.

Part 3:
Retiring with Spirit

In the twilight zone

Kate Taylor

Since I am past eighty, I have to accept that I am entering the twilight zone. I am frustratingly deaf, inclined to need more sleep than I used to, nervous of driving any distance in the dark, and yet determined to remain active. Although I was baptised and confirmed in the Church of England, I have attended the Unitarian Westgate Chapel in Wakefield since 1975. It is my spiritual home. The weekly services charge my batteries. In particular the words of some of our hymns provide the underpinning of my life. The Wakefield congregation regards a hymn by John White Chadwick (1840–1904) as its own anthem. It celebrates Unitarian faith:

> *O may that faith our hearts inspire*
> *To earnest thought and labour,*
> *That we may share its heavenly fire*
> *With every friend and neighbour:*
> *'Tis faith in God, and in ourselves,*
> *'Tis faith in truth and beauty,*
> *In freedom's might and reason's right,*
> *And all-controlling duty.*

Many Unitarian hymns celebrate our commitment to action, for our concern is much more about making a positive contribution to this world than seeking a place in a doubtful next one. I may be old, but the words of another American Unitarian, Love Maria Willis (1824–1908), still resonate as they have done for more than 45 years:

> *Hear, O God, the prayer we offer:*
> *Not for ease that prayer shall be,*
> *But for strength that we may ever*
> *Live our lives courageously.*

James Luther Adams, the American Unitarian Universalist theologian (1901–1994), remarked on the experiences that are possible 'only in fruited old age'. He spoke of 'the contemplation of satisfactions and beauties of long ago, the cherishing of old friendships, the exploration of opportunities previously unheeded', and 'the meeting of the adversity of ill health...with serenity and dignity'. I buy all of that. Perhaps, now that I am retired from all salaried professional demands, it is the chance to explore fresh opportunities that has the greatest appeal.

The joys of research

I find contentment in my twilight years in undertaking research, writing, and giving talks. Fresh opportunities do occur. Some months ago – perhaps because I had written a book about Wakefield in the nineteenth century – I was asked by the chairman of a local engineering firm to write the history of his 190-year old company, which began in 1824 by making hand-operated machines to form metals into milk churns and has developed into making machines to form superplastics for aeroplane parts. It has an annual turnover of £30m and exports to countries across the world. I accepted the challenge, and for some months I spent half a day a week in the firm's board room, making notes on my laptop from papers in its archives. The work took me to libraries, primarily to read nineteenth-century newspapers, and to the Leeds and Wakefield branches of the West Yorkshire Archive Service. Research into the context in which the firm has operated has been done via the internet. It was an entirely new field for me, but I think that wanting to know more, to understand, is a Unitarian characteristic. I have explored the early industrial exhibitions of the mid-nineteenth century and the great British Empire Exhibition of 1924, where the firm spent nearly £300 on its stand. I have learned about the impact of a moulders' strike, the three-day week of 1974, Britain's entry into the EEC, the move from iron to steel, the effect of changes in the value of the pound, and much more. The firm was the subject of a management buy-out from the Hanson Trust in 1984, hence I have begun to understand the reasons for the wave of buy-outs in the 1980s and the follies (as they seem to me) of Lord Hanson's industrial philosophy.

Deafness is no handicap to research if one's sources are written material. Problems arise when it is living people who hold the information that you want. The chairman of the engineering company, with great courtesy, always looked in on the board room when I was working there. He was happy to talk to me for hours about the firm's past and its achievements, but I could hear little of what he said. I would edge my chair closer to him and cup one of my ears, but he would raise his voice only momentarily. I took to sending him questions by e-mail on the days when I was not at the factory, in order to get written answers.

Chairing meetings, raising money, stuffing envelopes ...

My great achievement at Westgate Unitarian Chapel, where I am the chair of the trustees, is to have raised the funding and organised the reinstatement of our magnificent historic organ. Other than the regular but never very exacting demands of my commitment to the Chapel, I am kept very active as the chair, and effectively the administrator, of the Friends of Wakefield Chantry Chapel. This is one of only three remaining chapels in the whole country that were built on (rather than beside) bridges. It originated in the mid-fourteenth century, but its upper part – the worship area – was rebuilt, to the design of George Gilbert Scott, in the 1840s, when the building was reclaimed for the Church of England and became a chapel-of-ease for the newly formed parish of St Mary. Scott chose oolitic limestone from Bath and Caen (France), which deteriorates steadily in the Wakefield atmosphere. Major repairs took place in the 1880s, the 1930s, and the 1960s. By 1989 the chapel required some £100,000 for further extensive repairs. Its Parochial Church Council could not afford such a sum and, in any case, being of a low-church inclination, wanted to divest itself of the quaint and costly building. A group of Friends was formed as a registered charity with the two aims of keeping the building in good repair and making it better known to the wider public.

I joined the group as its press officer. Members of the management committee included our first Chair, who was very active in the United Reformed Church, plus a Roman Catholic, and a second Unitarian. We were all drawn to the project not because the chapel had originated as a mass house to say prayers for souls in Purgatory (why would we?), but because, with its bridge, it is a scheduled ancient monument with a fascinating history and is a significant part of Wakefield's heritage. It is, too, a beauty 'of long ago', although I do not think that that is what James Luther Adams had in mind. We raised and spent the £100,000, replacing the worn stone where necessary, rewiring the chapel, and installing a good heating system and new lighting. In 2000, the fully repaired Chantry was taken into the care of the Dean and Chapter of Wakefield Cathedral.

Having the ecumenical outlook common to Unitarians has made it easy for me to relate to the Anglican clergy. It has also led me to support the nearby Baptist chapel in its scheme to hold a winter sleep-out on the bridge to draw attention to the plight of the local homeless: we opened the chapel overnight to provide hot drinks and a stall for Baptist buns. I arrange for the Roman Catholic Latin Mass Society to celebrate the Feast of the Assumption of the BVM (as they like to call the Virgin) in the chapel on 15 August each year, and they, in turn, fulfil the Friends' wish to mark the death of Richard Duke of York in the Battle of Wakefield on 30 December 1460 by providing a requiem mass which is both a reverent occasion and marvellous theatre.

I have written every newsletter since the Friends' group was formed – so far totalling 85. I stuff the envelopes and take them to the post. The central – and always urgent – task for the Friends is to raise money. We hold open days and organise talks, concerts, and occasional dramatic performances. I give many talks across the West Riding in return for donations to our funds. The building is kept in excellent order, as we respond promptly to the recommendations of our architect at each quinquennial inspection.

Deafness need not be a handicap

The best place for a deaf person at meetings is in the chair. I can say (as often as necessary), *'Do speak up – remember I am very deaf'*. And at a lecture, the best role for me is as the speaker, although I find it increasingly hard to stand up for the requisite hour. The challenge comes at the end when the person who is presiding asks if I will take any questions. I say very firmly to the audience, *'Yes, of course, but I shall not hear what you are saying'*. I then look for the raised hands and move over to be very close to the questioners. That way we get along swimmingly. It does not seem to stem the flow.

Being in the audience is another thing entirely. I receive invitations to a range of rather alluring events. I normally respond by e-mail, asking what arrangements there are for the deaf. Is there a hearing loop? It is regrettable that host institutions which understand the needs of wheelchair users make few concessions to the deaf. The worst occasions are when speakers decline the offer of a microphone because – so they say – they have a good voice. I am not afraid to interrupt them by saying, 'I can't hear you'.

Maintaining a small specialist garden

Some of my happiest times are spent in an activity which I do alone and where deafness is no handicap – although an ageing body is. I look after my 'hosta garden' in the grounds of Westgate Chapel. It is a narrow strip of land, a little over a yard in width, running the full length of the east side of the building. Some years ago I cleared it of nettles, docks, dandelions, and buddleia, and planted a variety of hostas. They flourish. Now it is a matter of getting down on my knees to pick out from between them the sycamore seedlings, foxgloves, and wild violets (for even these last are not allowed). Getting upright again is something of a challenge, but I use my bucket as a support. No one else is there to see the ungainly manoeuvres. But I would not mind if they did. When you are in the twilight zone, elegance (unlike keeping active) is not a priority.

Questions for discussion and reflection

1. Do the words of any particular hymn have special significance for you? Why do they have such resonance?

2. How far does your local community matter to you, and in what ways can you, or could you, contribute to its well-being?

3. *'Grow old along with me! The best is yet to be, the last of life for which the first was made'*, wrote Robert Browning. What for you will be, or are, the good things about being 'in the twilight zone'?

4. Is society better geared to providing for people with some disabilities rather than others?

5. Many historic buildings are in the care of such bodies as English Heritage, Historic Scotland, or the National Trust. What is to be said for or against their being financed by an *ad hoc* body of volunteers such as the Friends of Wakefield Chantry Chapel? Is this something expected of the so-called 'big society'?

The author

Derek McAuley, Chief Officer of the General Assembly of Unitarian and Free Christian Churches, writes: Kate Taylor died on 5 May 2015 during the production of this book, having encouraged the idea from the very beginning. Kate was a lecturer and journalist, as well as a prolific author on local and cinema history. She was a member of Westgate Chapel, Wakefield (www.ukunitarians.org.uk/wakefield), and an able worship leader. She edited *Marking the Days,* a book of occasional services, published by the Lindsey Press in 2006, and she inspired and led the Lindsey Press Panel for many years. She served on the Board of Directors of *The Inquirer* as well as being the Annual Meetings Press Officer. After her death, Kate's name appeared in the Queen's Birthday Honours List for 2015, honoured with the award of MBE 'For services to heritage and to the community in Wakefield, Yorkshire'. The award was presented to her son at a service in Wakefield Cathedral. Kate was an outspoken and indefatigable presence in our movement: she will be greatly missed.

Living the dying

Elizabeth Birtles

Aged seven, very ill in hospital, I woke up and asked the nurse where my little friend in the next bed had gone. When told that she had been moved somewhere else, I knew intuitively that I was being 'protected' from the truth of her death. A very clear memory of my rage at this act of adult evasion, which I experienced as dishonesty, has always fed my concern never to 'protect' anyone, even children, from a difficult truth.

Aged nine when my first grandparent died, I remember sitting with my mother as she wept for her father, and as she explained that it brought back memories of the death of her first husband. Without being able to articulate it, I was able to understand how a death reawakens all the other experiences of loss: this death was not hidden, it was real, it was truthful, it was natural, and I was not afraid.

As a 'child of the Unitarian manse', I grew up immersed in Unitarian values, in a family where the expression of religious values and feelings literally shaped the weeks of our lives. Questioning, imagination, reverence for life, a non-dogmatic approach, an appreciation of poetic and prophetic language, delight in the natural world, self-discipline, and a strong sense of personal responsibility were among the threads that were encouraged in me. The dance between the transcendence and the immanence of the divine was alive in me long before I knew the words. I learned the value of reflecting on my experience, and the felt presence of God came, it seemed naturally, to have primacy over any belief or teaching. A strong feeling and understanding had grown in me that there is a reality which is beyond my words and beyond my senses.

> *There is a deeper than the depth of things,*
> *a something that is impossible to conceive,*
> *impossible not to conceive,*
> *both a presence and an absence. ....*
> *..*

I am content to rest in its strength and insecurity.
There is a deeper than the depth of things.[1]

Accepting death

We are all living and dying. I do not know when my death will come, and because I embrace the not-knowing, I take it as my responsibility to prepare myself. Just as I accepted the precious gift of life in me, so I will accept my death. It may not be easy: some deaths are hard. But, however it will be for me, I choose to be open to the mystery of it. I want to prepare for death, not in the sense of trying to be in control, but in the sense of being ready to live my dying, opening to a vast unknown.

Encountering the wisdom and practices of Zen Buddhism, Tibetan Buddhism, Celtic spirituality, and Sufism over the past thirty years has been of immeasurable value to me. The words, for example, of Rumi, the Persian Sufi mystic poet, challenge and inspire me:

Death, like most phenomena,
will treat you the same way you have treated him;
with someone who has been friendly
he will be kind and amicable,
and with an enemy he will wage war.[2]

I am called to practise surrendering any expectation of being in control, and to practise resting with not-knowing. I am called to practise opening compassionately to the fear, the pain, and the suffering in myself and others. I am called to practise 'making friends with death'. I am called to live the mystery of my dying.

1 Richard Gilbert, *To Whom it May Concern* (First Unitarian Church, Rochester, New York, 1981) pp. 38–39.
2 An extract from verse 3439 in Mathnawi Book 3 (Rumi), quoted in *Rumi Day By Day* by Maryam Mafi (Hampton Roads Publishing, 2014).

I take it to be my responsibility to prepare for my dying and my death. I do not feel that I had a right to be born, hence I do not feel I have a right to die. I cannot envisage asking someone to assist in my dying. The timing and manner of my death will not be known until the event. Meanwhile I do feel that I have both the right and the responsibility to live to the full the gift that is my life and my dying.

As I am now in the last phase of my living, I am considering the reality of my dying, and how I may most fully live the ending of my life. I have found it helpful to use guided meditations as a way to practise dying. I have been led through the process in imagination a number of times and in various forms. Reflection, alone and with others, has enabled me to focus on what matters most to me. I am aware that there are different aspects to consider for the different possible stages: ageing, ailing, a terminal phase of months/weeks, and active dying (last days/hours).

Those close to me know how hard it will be for me to resist the pressure of the prevailing Western model of medicine, which emphasises diagnosis and treatment of signs and symptoms. All too easily we can be seduced into allowing the focus to be on the amazing details of options, innovative interventions, and laudable efforts to prolong life. I intend to be alert to the possibility of being 'caught up' in an avalanche of crises from which medicine can offer only brief and temporary rescue. This, for me, would be the 'outer' work. In the closing phase of my life I would choose to put my energy into the 'inner' work. I do not want to denigrate the achievements of the medical world: in particular I am profoundly grateful for the developments in pain management in palliative care. But I have seen that all too often dying and death are 'medicalised', and so I prepare myself to resist this. I do this by engaging the support of those close to me, by writing down my wishes in advance, by focusing on what I call the 'inner' work, and by sustaining the spiritual practices that affirm my choice, if possible, to die consciously, in a calm, quiet setting.

It is important to me that I am able to communicate, in advance, to those who are close to me, what I think will matter most to me when I am actively dying. Who is doing what? Where and how? People, place, sights, sounds, smells, tastes, touch have all been considered, described, and noted. Vital to me will be the easy, relaxed presence of those who have known me, who respect my choices, and who will honour, with me, 'a deeper than the depth of things'. I wish to have near me those who are willing to be open to all the fears and pain, all the naturalness of processes, all the not-knowing, and all the mess, struggle, and suffering *in everyone present*. How wonderful it would be to be surrounded in my last days by some of those with whom I have practised surrendering any expectations of being in control! How wonderful it would be to hear some of the chants we have sung together, and to be resting in the presence of friends practising meditation, resting in the presence of Mystery!

While I am not afraid of dying, I have been haunted by the dread of dying *suddenly*. It is the inner work of meeting and embracing the fear of sudden death that has fuelled my focus on preparing for death. Letting go of the prospect of having time for final arrangements, letting go of the possibility of final goodbyes, letting go of the fear of leaving behind a disorganised mess: this has all been difficult. But the fears no longer paralyse me: every time a fear arises, I practise noticing it and letting it go. I practise connecting with a spirit of love and compassion in and around me, and I observe the fear evaporating. I remember the words of Elisabeth Kubler-Ross: '*When we are in a place of love, we cannot be in a place of fear.*'

I now accept that I may well not be able to die consciously in a quiet calm setting, in the easy relaxed presence of those who have known me.

Accompanying the dying

I have been immeasurably privileged to accompany a number of people as they lived their dying, and every time I have been aware that we were in the presence of 'a deeper than the depth of things'. This did not need to be articulated: it was palpable. Just before I enter a room where someone is dying, I pause. I breathe in a relaxed, natural way. I let go of all expectations. I reconnect with a felt sense of Light and Love, with openness, clarity and spaciousness, with Oneness. I enter the room with a willingness to be led by the person who is dying. I allow myself to be led. Why on earth would I know how this person will do his/her dying, any more than he/she knows? We are both in unknown territory, both entering Mystery. I trust the inner wisdom of the person, even though he/she may feel unable to do so. While I am holding the thread of that trust – holding it for him or her – and holding it in the spirit of love and compassion, then I am not carrying fear into the room.

> A dying person most needs to be shown as unconditional love as possible, released from all expectations. Don't think you have to be an expert in any way. Be natural, be yourself, be a true friend, and the dying person will be reassured that you are really with them, communicating with them simply and as an equal, as one human being to another.[3]

I have been present with a dying person as a daughter, a cousin, a niece, a friend, a colleague, a minister, a covenant companion. Possibly more than at any other time, these were the days and hours when concepts of role were irrelevant: we were simply human beings. In the presence of the person who is dying, I am a human being who supports her in the journey she is making; and every journey is unique. I support her best, I think, by being alongside her as often as she wants, by being relaxed and open to whatever comes, by being fully present to her and her experience, by being guided by her, and by trusting the process even when she cannot.

Sometimes there are words, sometimes there is silence. There may be long minutes, hours, days of waiting and watching and listening. Sometimes I breathe with her, following her rhythm. My focus is always on her. And at the same time, as often as possible, I am monitoring my own responses to what comes. As feelings sweep through me, I observe them, and let them go.

Always my focus is on her. There may be anger, frustration, denial, guilt, indignity, incoherence, quiet conversation, poetry, horrifying moments, sudden expressions of deep fear or sadness, quiet resting, agitation, little worries, laughter, the need for forgiveness /reassurance/ reconciliation, spells of practical planning, interruptions, anguish, sleeping, dreaming.

---

3   Sogyal Rinpoche, *The Tibetan Book of Living and Dying* (HarperCollins, 1992).

... Whatever comes, I trust her inner wisdom: I honour her way of living her dying.

> ... in the shared embrace of meditation, a caregiver and dying person can be held in an intimate silence beyond consolation or assistance. When sitting with a dying person, I try to ask myself carefully, What words will benefit her? Does anything really need to be said? Can I know greater intimacy with her through a mutuality beyond words and actions? Can I relax and trust in simply being here, without needing my personality to mediate the tender connection we share? [4]

With shame I acknowledge that, for me, one of the greatest challenges to being present with a dying person has been the time when there have been other people in or near the room. I have found it quite difficult to do what might be described as the delicate dance between the person who is dying and others. Family members, friends, medical professionals may come in with very different concerns, hopes, expectations, and very different ways of being. With my focus on the dying person, there has been little space, time, or energy for me to respond even adequately to these others. I regret my failures to 'do the dance'. I have tried to make amends by giving the others attention outside the room. And I resolve to continue to practise recognising my irritation/ frustration/ anger/ disappointment with others, and then letting those feelings go, opening my heart to them generously when they are in the room. I will need to cultivate the capacity to expand my focus to include every one.

Conclusion

I wonder if anything that I have written will 'speak' to you, will encourage you, will help you find *your* wisdom? I hope so. But I don't know. And I

---

4   Joan Halifax, *Being With Dying: Cultivating Compassion and Fearlessness in the Presence of Death* (Shambhala Publications, 2009).

recall that Henri Nouwen tells us: 'Befriending our death is a life-long spiritual task'.

And so I return to my practice of resting with not-knowing, resting with Mystery.

> *Nothing is lost; be still; the universe is honest.*
> *Time, like the sea, gives it all back in the end,*
> *But only in its own way, on its own conditions:*
> *Empires as grains of sand, forests as coal,*
> *Mountains as pebbles. Be still, be still, I say;*
> *You were never the water, only a wave:*
> *Not substance, but a form substance assumed.*
> (Elder Olson[5])

Yes, we are like waves: we are given shape and form, and then that form begins to dissolve. And what we are in essence returns to be part of the greater mystery of the sea.

> *Everything you see has its roots in the unseen world.*
> *The forms may change, yet the essence remains the same.*
> *Every wonderful sight will vanish, every sweet word will fade,*
> *But do not be disheartened:*
> *The source they come from is eternal, growing,*
> *Branching out, giving new life and new joy.*
> *Why do you weep?*
> *The source is within you*
> *And this whole world is springing up from it.*[6]
> (Mevlana Jelaluddin Rumi)

5   From 'The Exegesis' by Elder Olson, quoted in *Great Occasions*, edited by Carl Seaburg (Skinner House, 1988).
6   Quoted in *The Way Of Passion: A Celebration Of Rumi* by Andrew Harvey (Frog Ltd, Berkeley, CA, 1994, p. 189).

Questions for discussion and reflection

In my experience, it is natural for our views of our living and dying to evolve and change over time. I have found it enormously helpful to ponder certain questions privately and with others, in the context of well-facilitated small groups built on trust. So here are a few questions to reflect on.

1. What do you expect will be the most difficult aspects to encounter in your dying and death?
2. What is important to you as you move towards your dying and your death? Are you able to share these realisations with those close to you?
3. Who do you want to make decisions for you if you can't make them for yourself?
4. If you receive a diagnosis of terminal illness, how much are you willing to go through to stay alive?
5. When your death comes, what do you NOT want to happen?
6. What do you need to do now to prepare for your dying and your death?
7. What do you need to do now to prepare for the dying and the death of those close to you?
8. What do you think and feel about being assisted in your dying?
9. How will it be for you if someone asks you to assist in his/her dying?
10. What are your beliefs about death? Can you trace their origins? Have they changed?
11. What gives you the greatest solace when you face the pain of loss and ending?
12. How are you best supported in a time of uncertainty?

Further reading

Coberley, Margaret (2003) *Sacred Passage: How to Provide Fearless Compassionate Care for the Dying*, Boston, MA: Shambhala Publications.

Gawande, Atul (2014) *Being Mortal: Medicine and What Matters In The End*, New York: Metropolitan Books/Henry Holt.

Glassman, Bernie (1999) *Bearing Witness: A Zen Master's Lessons in Making Peace*, Harmony/Bell Tower.

Halifax, Joan (2009) *Being With Dying: Cultivating Compassion and Fearlessness in the Presence of Death*, Boston, MA: Shambhala Publications.

Kearney, Michael (2000) *A Place of Healing: Working with Suffering in Living and Dying*, Oxford: Oxford University Press.

Kubler-Ross, Elisabeth (1970) *On Death and Dying*, New York: Simon & Schuster/Touchstone.

Kubler-Ross, Elisabeth and David Kessler (2000) *Life Lessons: How our Mortality Can Teach us about Life and Living*, New York: Simon & Schuster.

Levine, Stephen (1988) *Who Dies? An Investigation of Conscious Living and Conscious Dying*, Enfield: Airlift.

Levine, Stephen (1998) *A Year to Live: How to Live This Year As If It Were Your Last*, Bell Tower.

Nouwen, Henri (1994) *Our Greatest Gift: A Meditation on Dying and Caring*, SanFrancisco: Harper.

Rinpoche, Sogyal (1992) *The Tibetan Book of Living and Dying*, New York: HarperCollins.

The author

Elizabeth Birtles writes: 'Born in Southport, Lancashire, in 1949, I grew up in Bristol and Birmingham, where my father was a Unitarian minister. As the 1960s ended, I studied for an External London General BA in English, Philosophy & Theology at Manchester College, Oxford, and then did postgraduate teacher training in Walsall. After a year spent teaching in Ghana with Voluntary Service Overseas, I began teaching in Stockport.

'Seventeen years in teaching and then seventeen years in Unitarian ministry have shaped me. The other experiences that have strongly shaped me include nine years' training towards an Advanced Diploma in Psychodynamic Counselling; thirty years' meditation practice; a passion for working in depth with small groups; divorce, separation, and loss; being part of Unitarian, Quaker, and Sufi communities; engaging in mentoring relationships; a love of walking and fresh air; poetry; and membership of a covenanted group of Unitarian colleagues.'

Lightning Source UK Ltd.
Milton Keynes UK
UKOW01f2354060416

271709UK00001BA/37/P

9 780853 190882